Paint Shop Pro 2021 Fundamentals

by Len Nasman

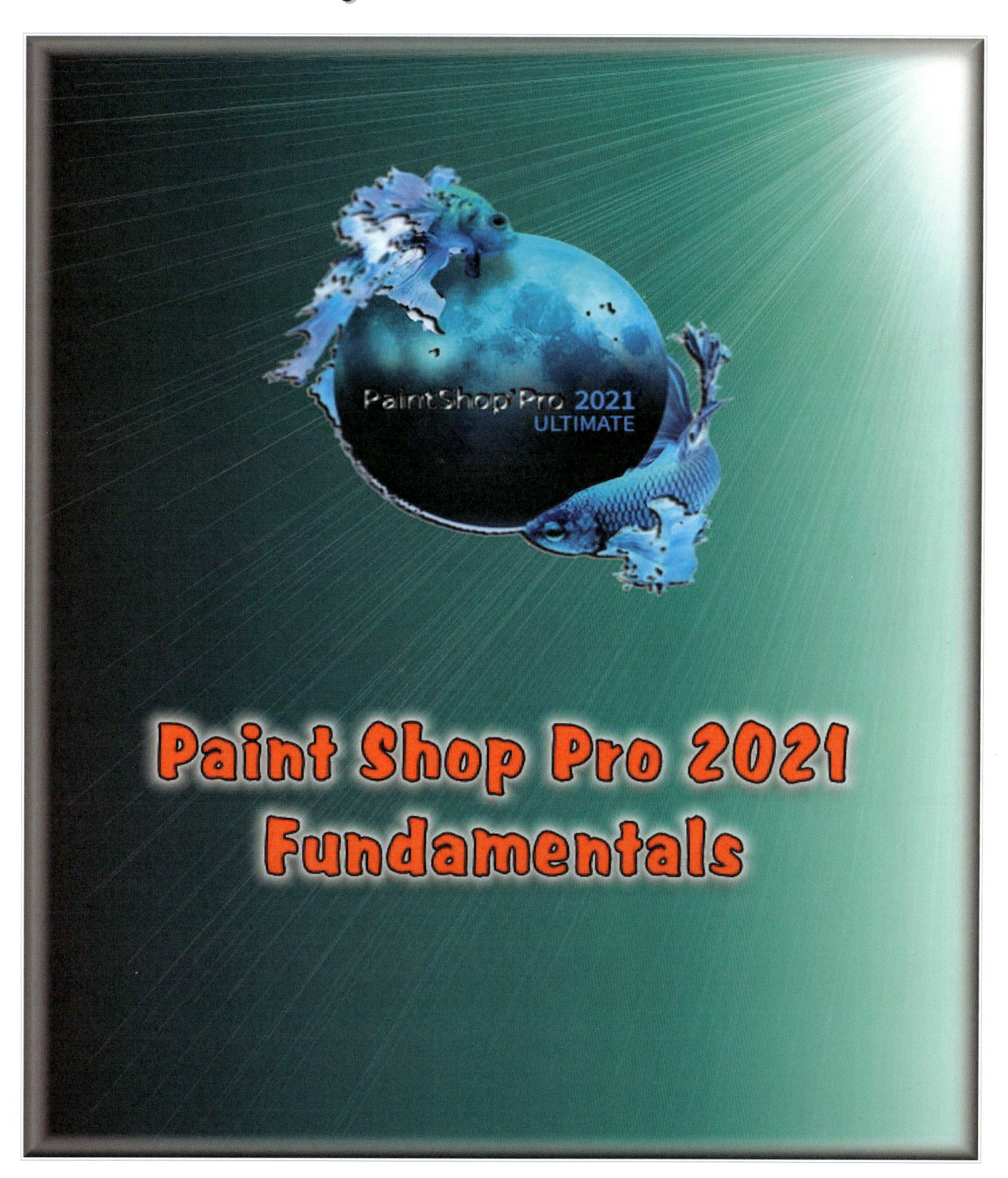

Paint Shop Pro 2021 Fundamentals

BVCC

PaintShop Pro 2021 ULTIMATE

Copyright 2021
by Len Nasman
All rights reserved

NOTE: A set of YouTube videos that are closely coordinated with this document is available. Open your web browser and search for **learnatlenshamn**.

Paint Shop Pro 2021 Fundamentals

Table of Contents

Part 1 - Drawing..5

Introduction..5
The Paint Shop Pro 2021 Welcome Screen..5
Workspace Options..6
Creating a New Document..7
The Paint Shop Pro User Interface..8
Using the Paint Brush Tool..9
Raster vs Vector Objects..11
Creating Vector Objects..12
Creating Text..15
Adding Text..15
Adding a Drop Shadow to Text..17
Modifying a Text Layer...18
Text Cutter Tool...20
Creating Curved Text...21
Picture Tube Fun..22
The Flood Fill Tool...23

Part 2 – Enhancing Photos..24

Enhancing Photos..24
Cropping Images..24
Adding Picture Frames...28
Straighten and Perspective Correction Tools......................................29
Resizing Images...31
Enhancing Images..34
Adjusting Brightness and Contrast..35
The Vibrancy Tool..36
One Step Noise Removal...37
The Lighten/Darken tool..38
The Scratch Remover Tool..39
Th Background Eraser tool..42
The Object Remover Tool..44

Paint Shop Pro 2021 Fundamentals

Part 3 - Printing..48
Printing Images..48
The Print Dialog Box Options...48
Custom Print Layouts..50

Part 4 - Customizing The Interface, And Tips And Tricks....................52
Creating A Custom Toolbar and Workspace...................................52
Saving A Workspace..53
Tips and Tricks..54

Enhancing Photos

Part 1 - Drawing

Introduction

Paint Shop Pro 2021 is a very powerful image processing and paint program. Although it has most of the common features of the much more expensive Adobe Photoshop, many users find Paint Shop Pro 2021 much easier to learn. This tutorial will focus on some commonly used features of Paint Shop Pro 2021. Many of the features covered are also common to earlier versions of Paint Shop Pro.

In the earliest versions of Paint Shop Pro, the focus was on creating drawings. As the program evolved, it gravitated toward modifying and enhancing photo images. However, all of the core drawing tools remain. In this tutorial, we will start with some common drawing features, and then move on to modifying and enhancing photos in later sections.

> **An associated set of videos for this book can be found at:**
> http://lenshamn.com/learnatlenshamn.html

The Paint Shop Pro 2021 Welcome Screen

✓ **Open Paint Shop Pro 2021.**

When Paint Shop Pro 2021 is opened, the **Welcome Screen** will appear. (If this is not the first time the program has been opened, you can go to the **Welcome Screen** by selecting the **Home** tool.

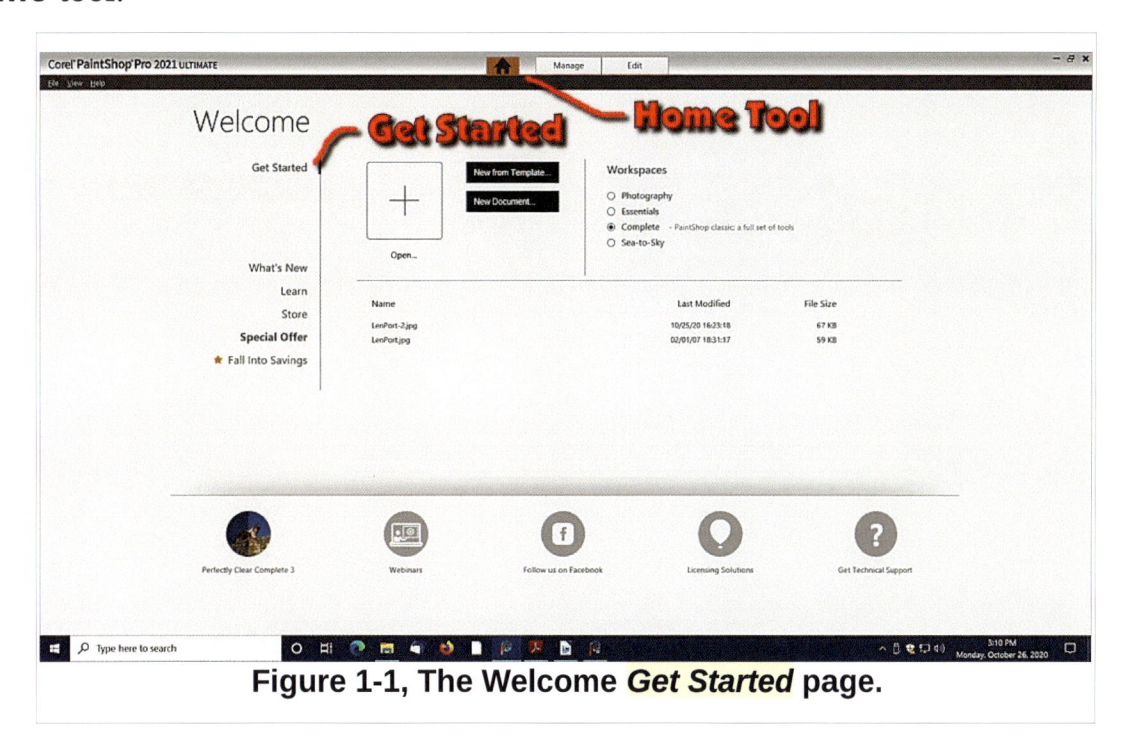

Figure 1-1, The Welcome *Get Started* page.

Paint Shop Pro 2021 Fundamentals

Observe the column below the **Get Started** entry (see Figure 1-1). Selecting each of these will open a different **Welcome** screen page.

> ✓ Explore the different Welcome screen pages.

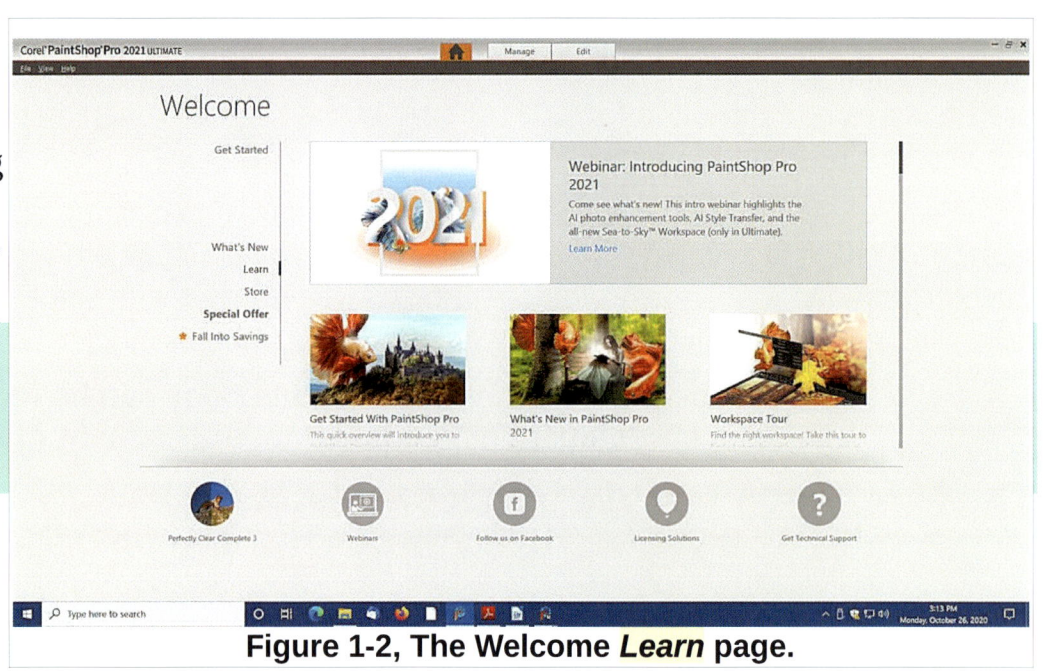

Figure 1-2, The Welcome *Learn* page.

Workspace Options

The **Welcome** screen **Get Started** page lists several **Workspace** options. The default options are provided for the different types of documents to be created or modified. As you gain experience with the program, you will probably create your own custom **Workspaces**.

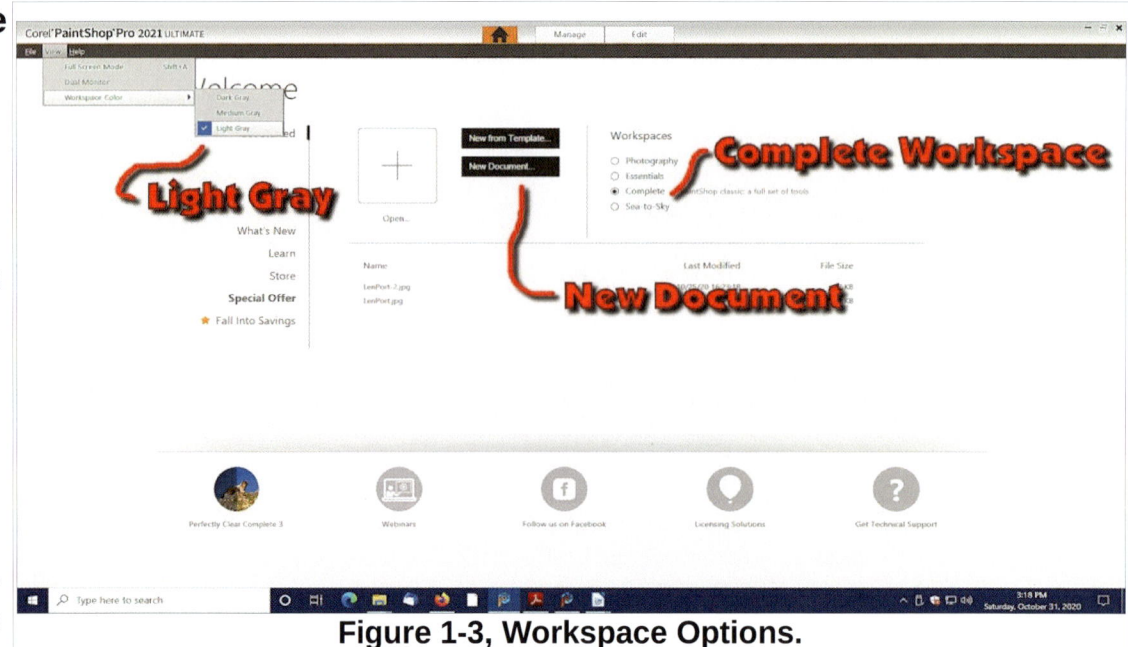

In the first example, we will use the **Complete** *Workplace option*.

Figure 1-3, Workspace Options.

Part 1 - Drawing

Creating a New Document

- From the *Menubar*, select **View, Workspace Color, Light Gray**.
- In the Welcome Get Started page, select the **Complete** *Workspace option*, and then select **New Document**.

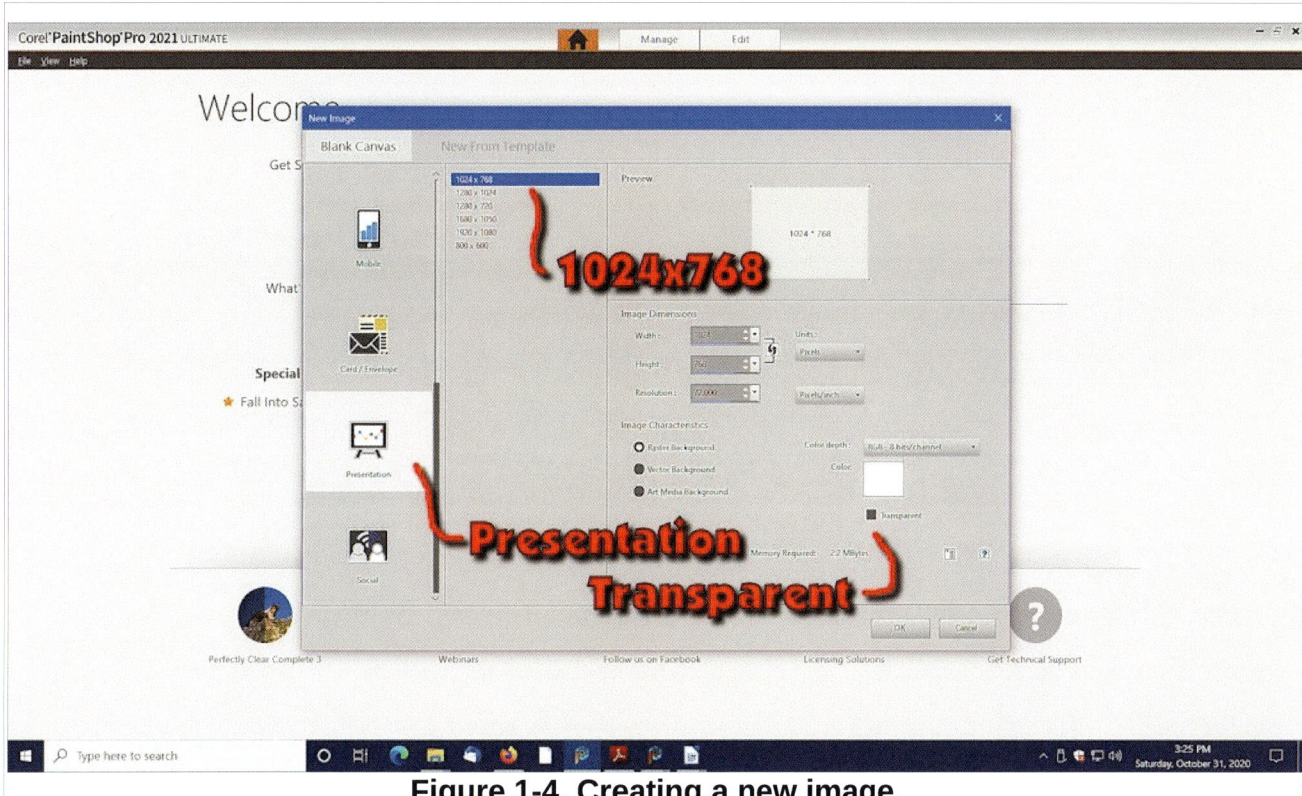

Figure 1-4, Creating a new image.

To keep the file size small, we will create a new image that has a 1024x768 resolution.

- In the *New Image* dialog box, select the **Presentation** *Blank Canvas* option.
- Set the *resolution* to **1024x768**.
- Toggle *Transparency* **off**, and then select **OK**.

Paint Shop Pro 2021 Fundamentals

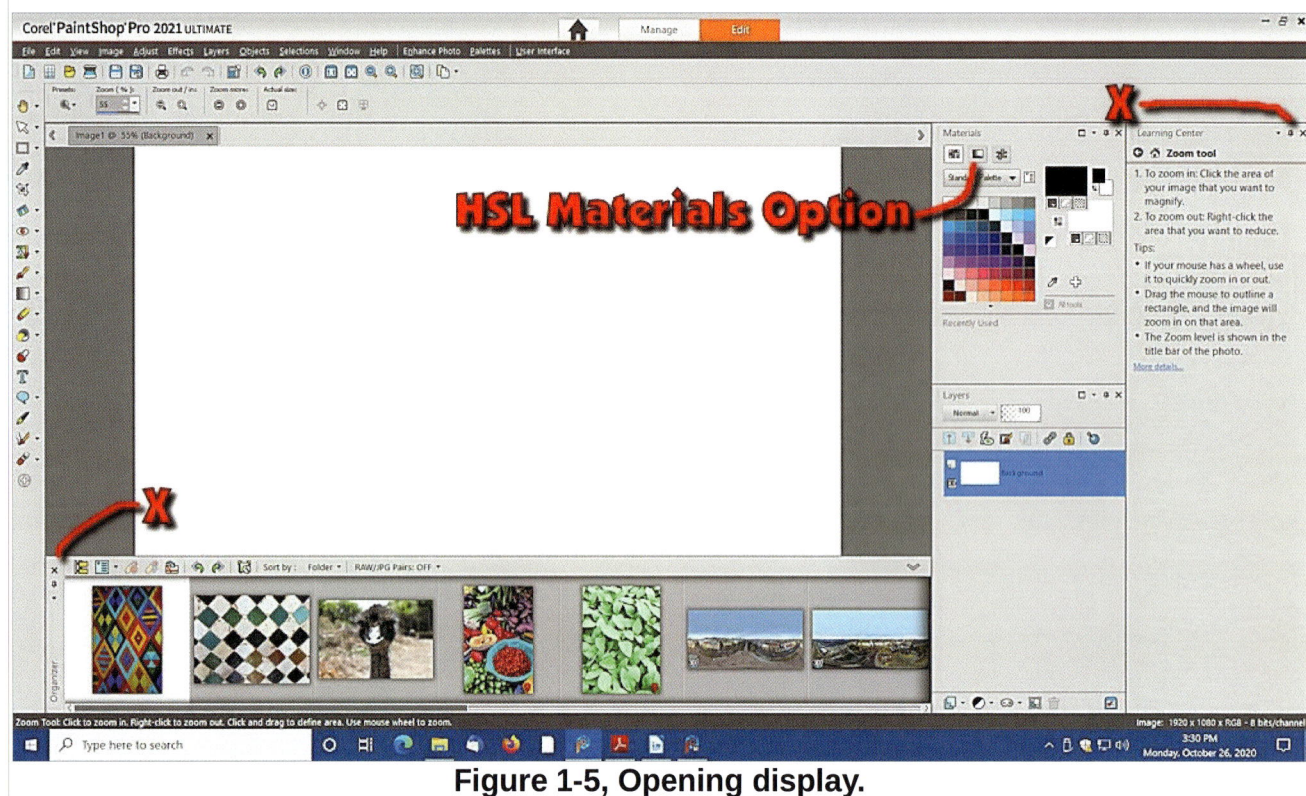

Figure 1-5, Opening display.

This will open the image in the default opening screen. The **Organizer** and **Learning Center** Palettes will not be used in this exercise, so they will be turned off.

- Turn off the **Organizer** and **Learning Center** palettes.

Palettes can be turned on and off from the **Menubar** by selecting **View, Palettes**.

There are several **Materials** options available. In this example, we will use the **ISL** option. Figure 1-5 shows how to select the **Materials**.

- In the **Materials** area, select the **ISL** option.

The Paint Shop Pro User Interface

- Figure 1-6 shows the user interface. Observe some of the interface areas.

Part 1 - Drawing

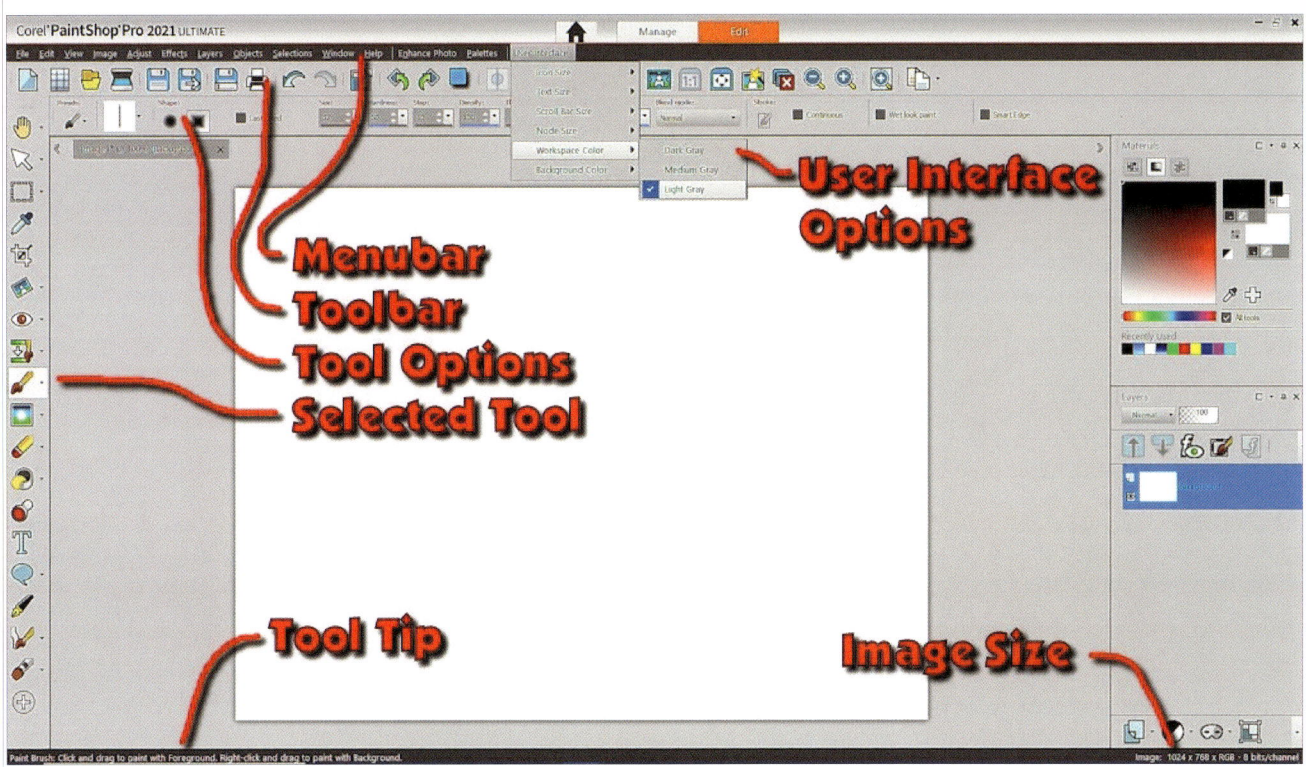

Figure 1-6, The User Interface.

The **Menubar** provides pop down lists of options. Observe the **User Interface** options shown in Figure 1-6.

- ✓ Select **User Interface** from the **Menubar** and select your preferred **Icon Size** and **Workspace Color**.

The **Toolbar** provides a selection of common tools. The **Toolbar** can be customized to include your favorite tools. How to customize the **Toolbar** will be shown later in this document.

The **Tool Options** will change when different tools are selected from the list of tools. Figure 1-6 shows that the **Paint Brush** tool has been selected.

The bottom line of the display shows a **Tool Tip** for the selected tool. It also shows the **Size** of the current image.

Using the Paint Brush Tool

Next, the **Paint Brush** tool will be selected and a few lines will be drawn.

> To draw with the **Paint Brush** tool position the cursor at the desired starting point, hold the **left mouse button down**, move the cursor to the **ending point**, and then release the left mouse button.

- ✓ Select the **Paint Brush** tool and use the **Tool Options** to select a brush style.

Paint Shop Pro 2021 Fundamentals

✓ Draw several lines.

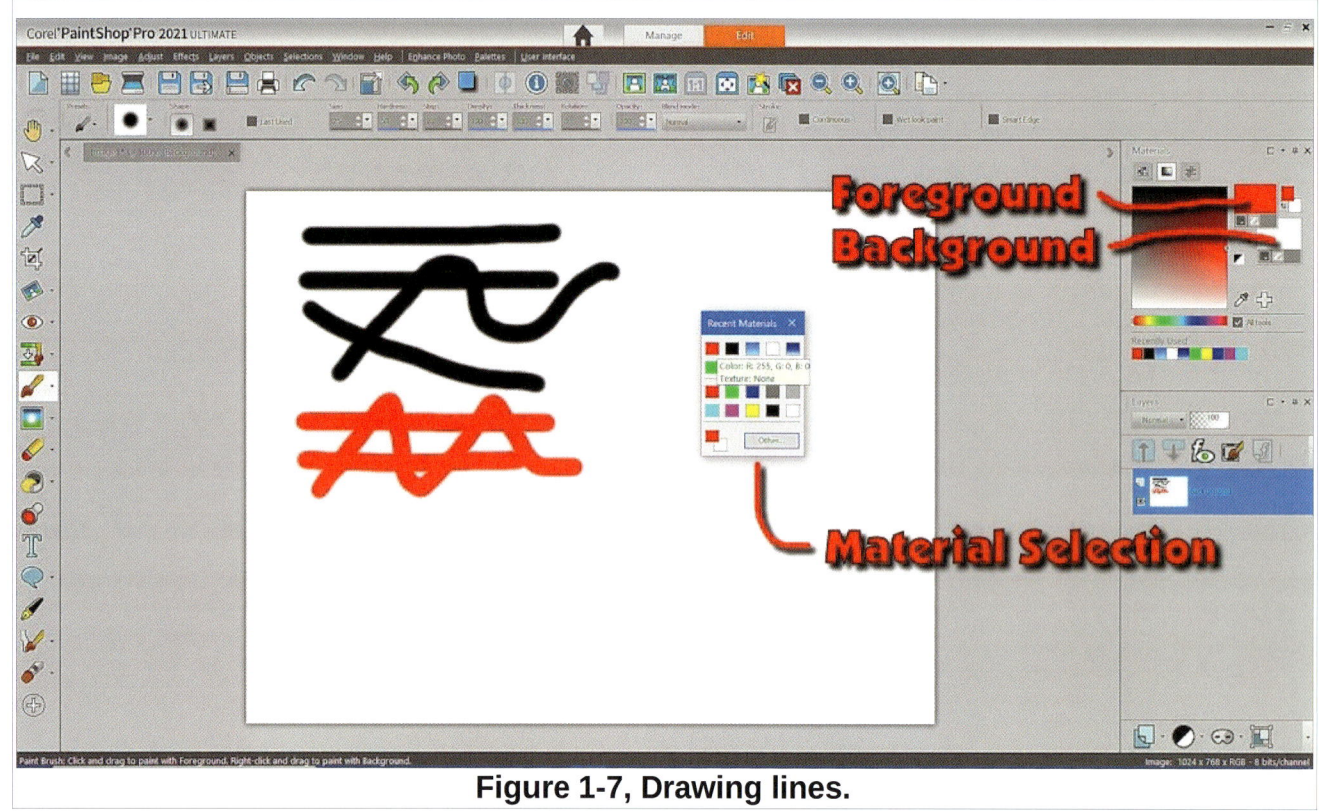

Figure 1-7, Drawing lines.

Figure 1-7 shows several lines. The foreground color can be selected several ways. One is to **left click** in the large material selection box. Figure 1-7 shows the **ISL Material** option.

> To change the range of the ISL Material, select a color from the color bar below the Material selection box.

To change the Foreground material color to a default color, **right click** on the foreground color box and then select a color from the material selection pop up window. You can also select a color from the Recently Used list.

✓ Experiment drawing with different foreground colors.
✓ Experiment with different Brush sizes and styles.

You can use the same technique to select the background color.

> Use the **left mouse button** to draw with the **foreground** color and use the **right mouse button** to draw with the **background** color.

✓ Select different foreground and background colors and experiment with drawing with the left and right mouse buttons,

Part 1 - Drawing

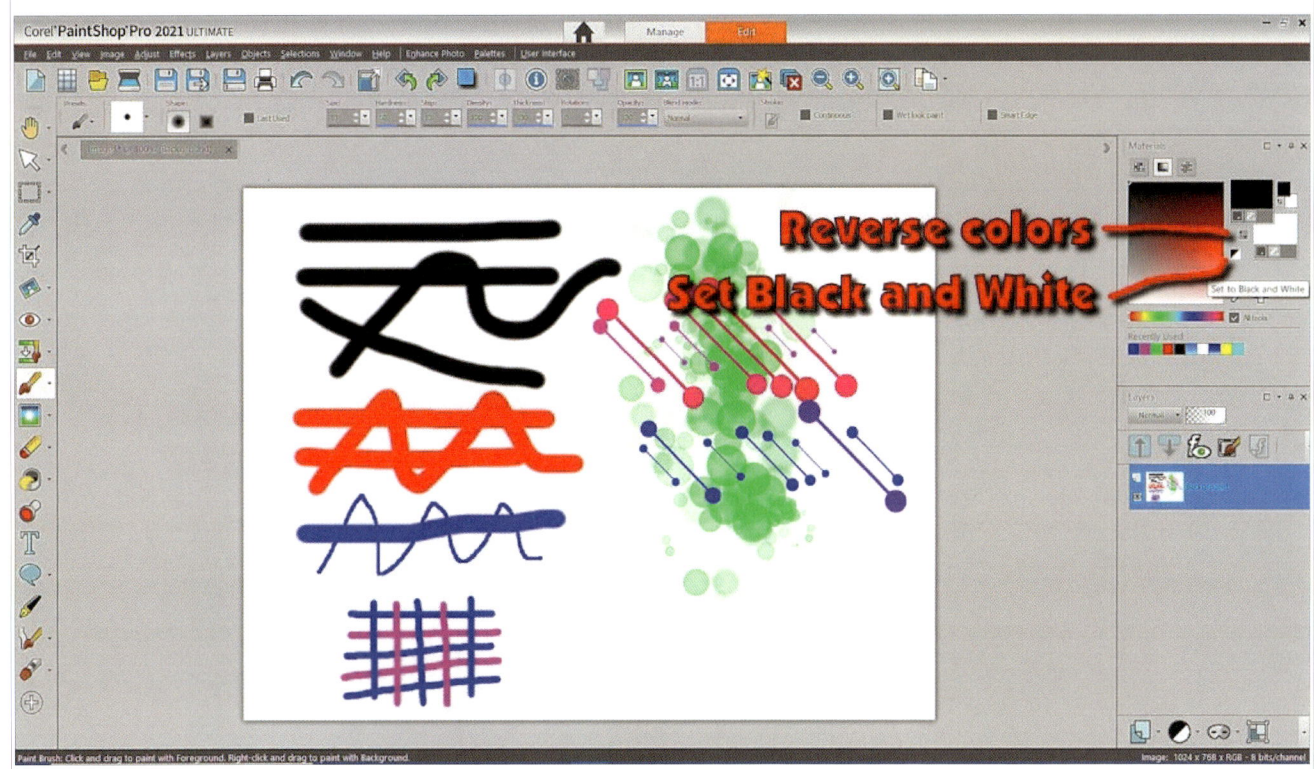

Figure 1-8, Drawing experiments.

Observe the two small tools in Figure 1-8. One is used to reverse the foreground and background colors. The other resets the colors to black and white.

- Experiment with reversing foreground and background tools.
- Reset the foreground and background colors to black and white.

To remove everything from the drawing, from the **Menubar** choose **Selections, Select All**. Press the **Delete** key. Then from the **Menubar** choose **Selections, Select None**. [Observe the shortcuts **Ctrl+A** and **Ctrl+D**.]

When you select all and press the Delete key, the system will replace everything with the current background color.

- Remove everything from your drawing. Then experiment with Paint Brush tools and foreground and background colors. Be sure to experiment with Hardness, Density, Thickness, and other options.
- When you have finished experimenting, reset the foreground and background to black and white, delete everything, and select None.

Raster vs Vector Objects

Raster vs Vector objects. There are two types of objects, *raster* and *vector*. When you were drawing with the Paint Brush tool earlier, you were creating raster images.

Paint Shop Pro 2021 Fundamentals

Raster images are collections of little square areas called pixels. If you zoom in on the drawing you made with the Paint Brush, you will see the individual pixels. The size of the pixels depends on the resolution of the image. If you enlarge a raster object, the pixels will be enlarged.

Vector objects use formulas rather than pixels to draw lines and curves. This means that when they are enlarged they take on the resolution of the display or printer.

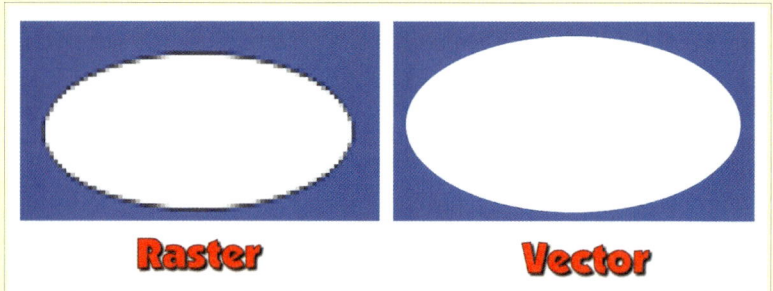

If you enlarge a curved raster object to the size of a billboard, the curves would be jagged. If you enlarge a vector object to the size of a billboard, the curved lines would be smooth.

Creating Vector Objects

When you add text to a drawing, the text is automatically created as a vector object. It is also placed on a different drawing layer, but more about layers later.

Paint Shop Pro has a number of other vector objects including **curved lines, preset shapes, Rectangles, Ellipse**, and **Symmetric Shape**.

Observe that when you select a Preset or other vector object tool, the context tool bar provides different options for creating the shape.

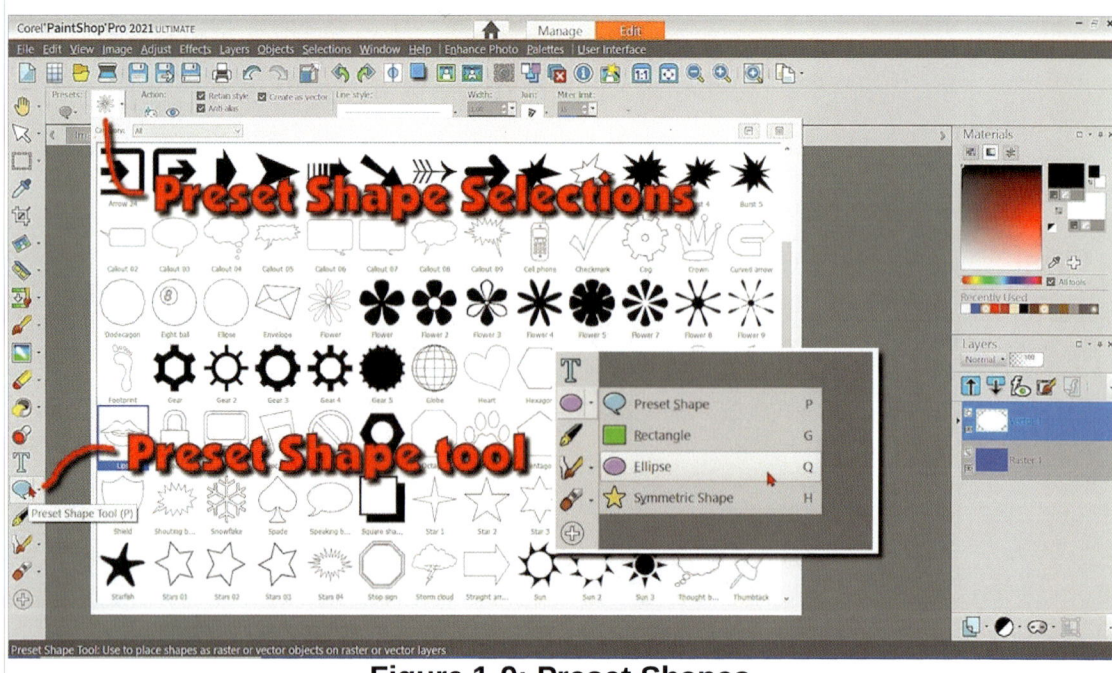

Figure 1-9: Preset Shapes

Part 1 - Drawing

- Open a new image and experiment with the different **Vector Preset Shapes**.
- Select the **Pick Tool**, then **Double click** on a vector object to open the **Vector Property** dialog box.

Figure 1-10: Preset Shapes.

Figure 1-11 shows the **Vector Property** dialog box.

The **Vector Property** dialog box can be used to change the stroke and fill properties of a vector object.

When a vector object is selected, the background color is the fill color for the object.

The **Pen Tool** can also be used to create vector objects. When the **Pen Tool** is selected, the context toolbar provides a number of different options.

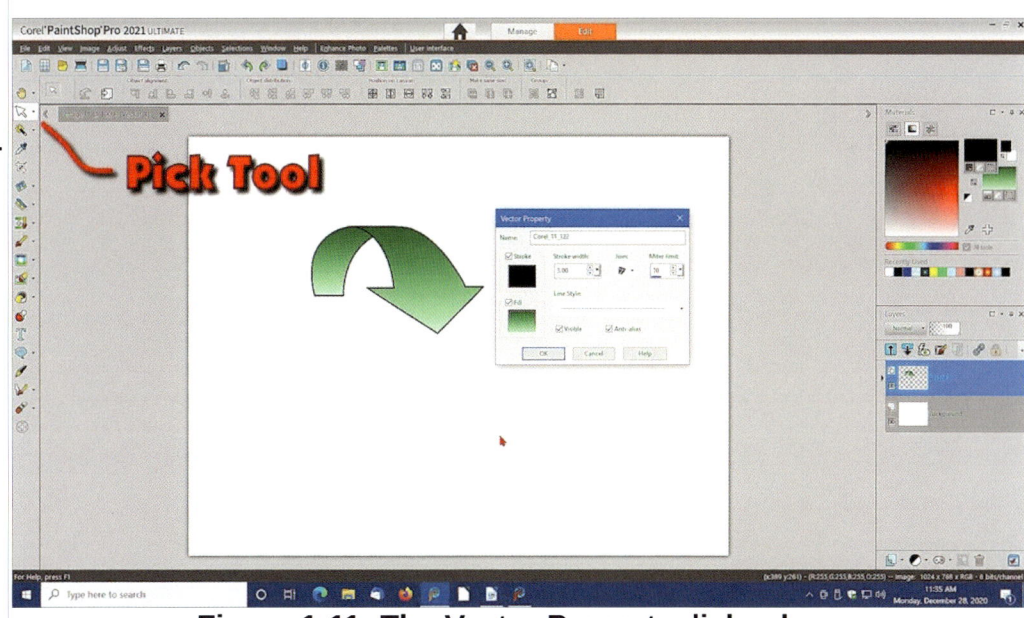

Figure 1-11: The Vector Property dialog box.

Page 13

Observe the Layers in Figure 1-12. The green Background is on a raster layer, while the text and vector objects are each on different layers. You can select a layer to edit things on that layer. There are a lot of things to learn about layers, however, a detailed discussion of layers is beyond the scope of this document.

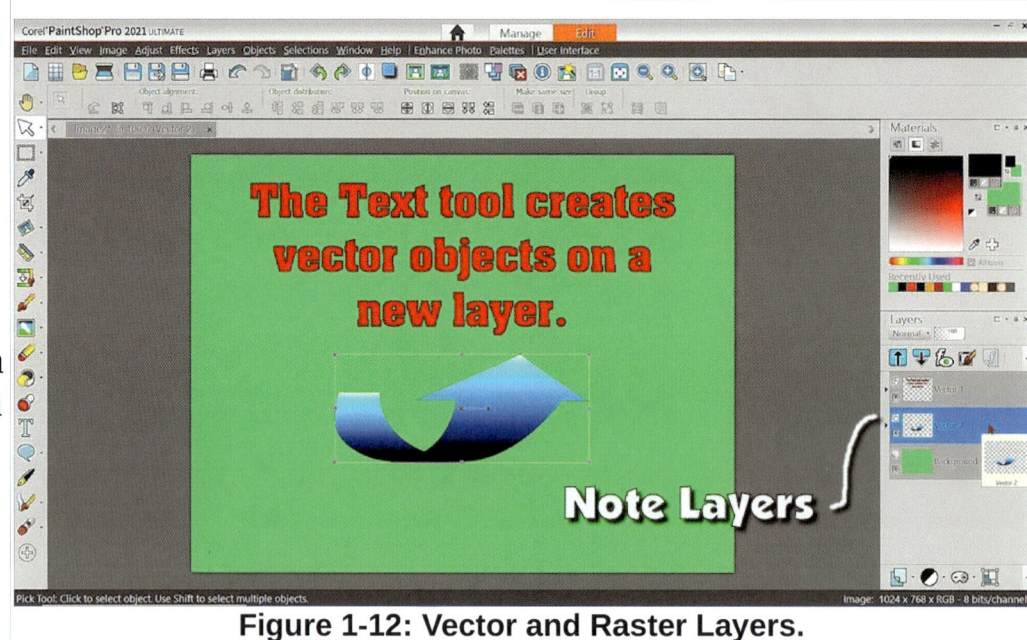

Figure 1-12: Vector and Raster Layers.

Part 1 - Drawing

Creating Text

The **Text** tool in Paint Shop Pro can be used to create signs, or to add text to photos or other graphic images. When the **Text** tool is selected, the **Context Toolbar** changes to text formatting tools that are similar to most word processing programs.

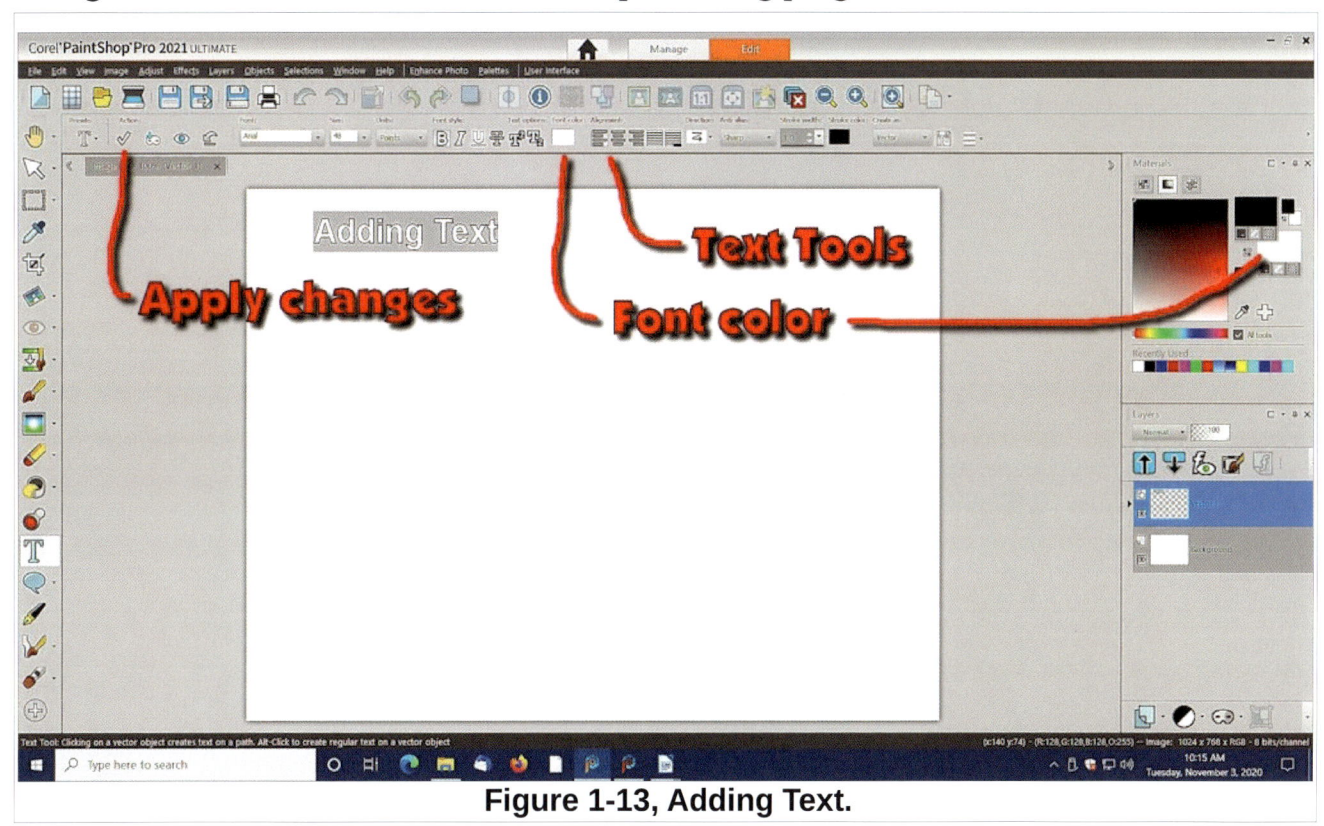

Figure 1-13, Adding Text.

✓ Open a new 1024x768 drawing.

Adding Text

Figure 1-13 was created by entering the words **Adding Text** using a font named **Arial** with the **Size** set to **48**.

Observe that there are tools in the **Context Toolbar** for setting justification to left, center, or right, similar to word processing software. These settings affect currently selected text entries. You can enter several different lines of text in the same text entry box by pressing the Enter key after each line.

Paint Shop Pro 2021 uses the **foreground** color for the border around the characters and the **background** color for the body of the characters.

> Left clicking on the **Font Color** tool in the Text Formatting Toolbar opens the **Materials Properties** dialog box, while right clicking opens a Recent Materials box.

Paint Shop Pro 2021 Fundamentals

> ✔ Select the **Text** tool, click at a location for the text, enter some text, then select the **Apply** changes tool.

When you select the **Apply changes** tool, the new text will be in a **text box**. You can use the grab points on the text box to resize the text box. When the four way arrow cursor is shown, you and drag the text box to a new location.

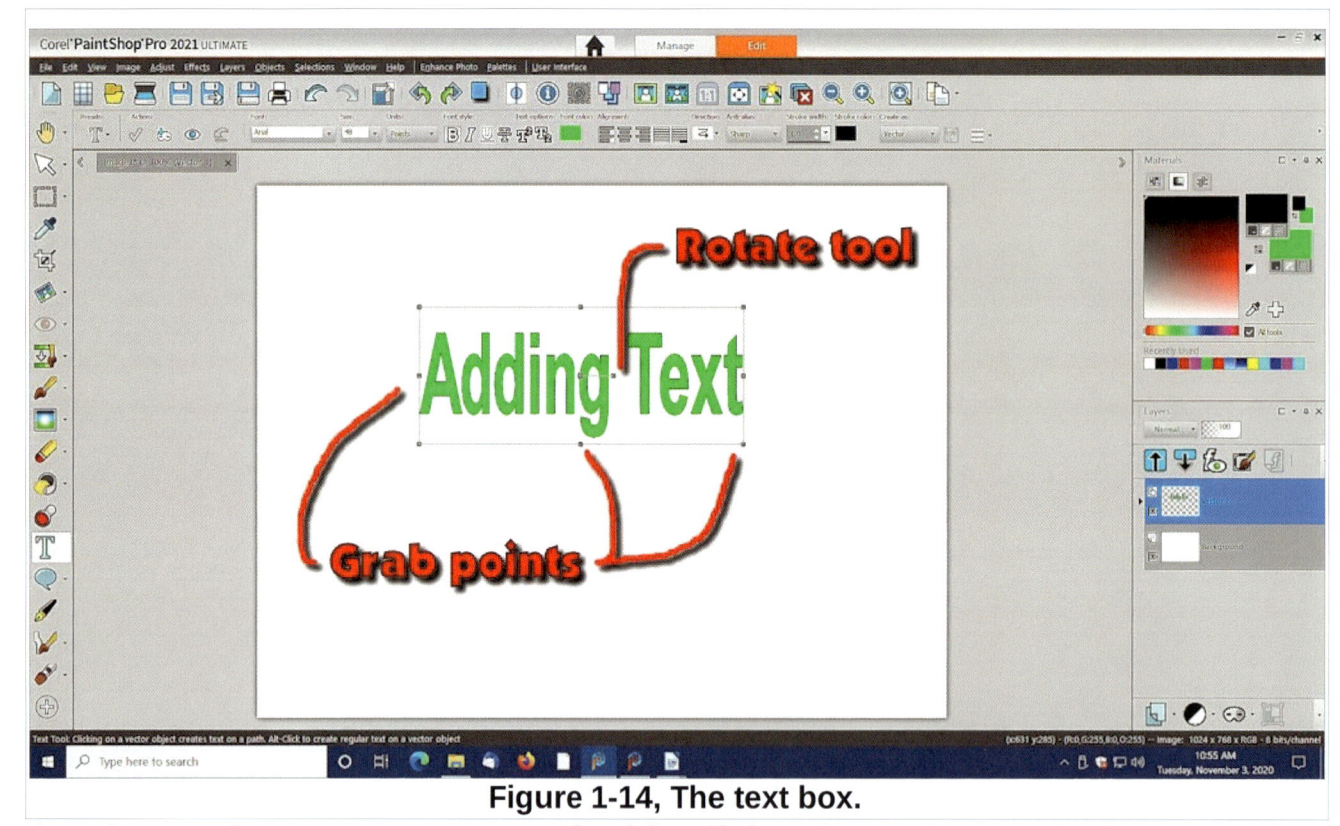

Figure 1-14, The text box.

When the **text box** is active, you can **double click** in the text box to edit the text. At the center of the selected text, there is a drag point. This can be used to drag the selected text to a new location. A rotate grab point can be used to rotate the text box.

> ✔ Add some text and experiment with the text box grab points.
> ✔ Drag text to a new location.
> ✔ Try rotating the text.

If you cannot place text, use the **Cancel changes** tool to remove any selected area.

When the text cursor is in the text box, you can use select all (**Ctrl+A**) or other text selection tricks (double or triple click) to select all or part of the current text. Use the **text tools** to adjust **selected** text.

> ✔ Experiment with the **Stroke width**.

Page 16

Part 1 - Drawing

- Use the **Stroke color** tool, or the **Foreground color** to change the **Stroke color**.
- Experiment with the **Stroke width**.

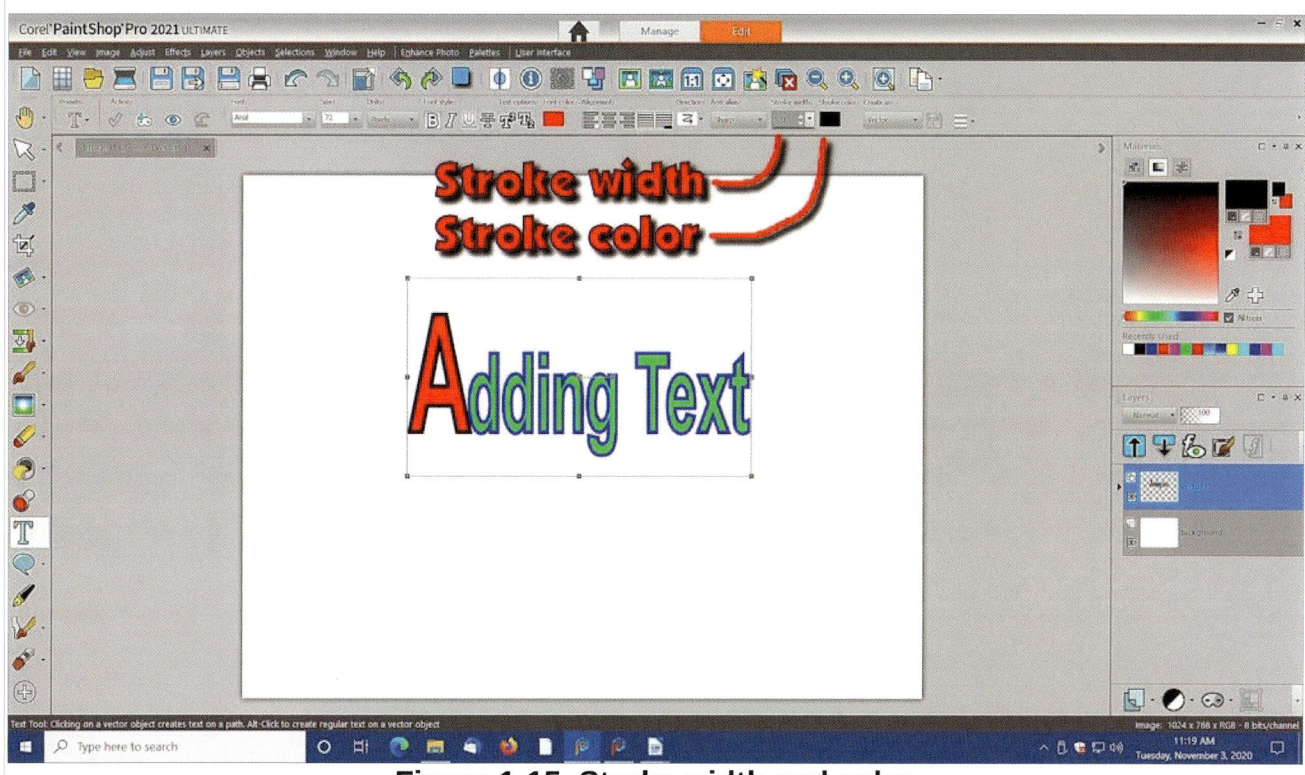

Figure 1-15, Stroke width and color.

Observe that the **stroke color** is the same as the **foreground color**. Figure 1-15 demonstrates that you can apply different fonts and colors to parts of the text by selecting individual parts of the text and applying different options.

Adding a Drop Shadow to Text.

Adding a drop shadow to text can enhance the text. Also, if the text is being placed over a graphic image, drop shadows can improve readability.

> **NOTE**: When a drop shadow is added to text, it will become a raster, rather than vector object.

- Create a new 1024x768 drawing.
- Add some text to the drawing similar to Figure 1-16.

Paint Shop Pro 2021 Fundamentals

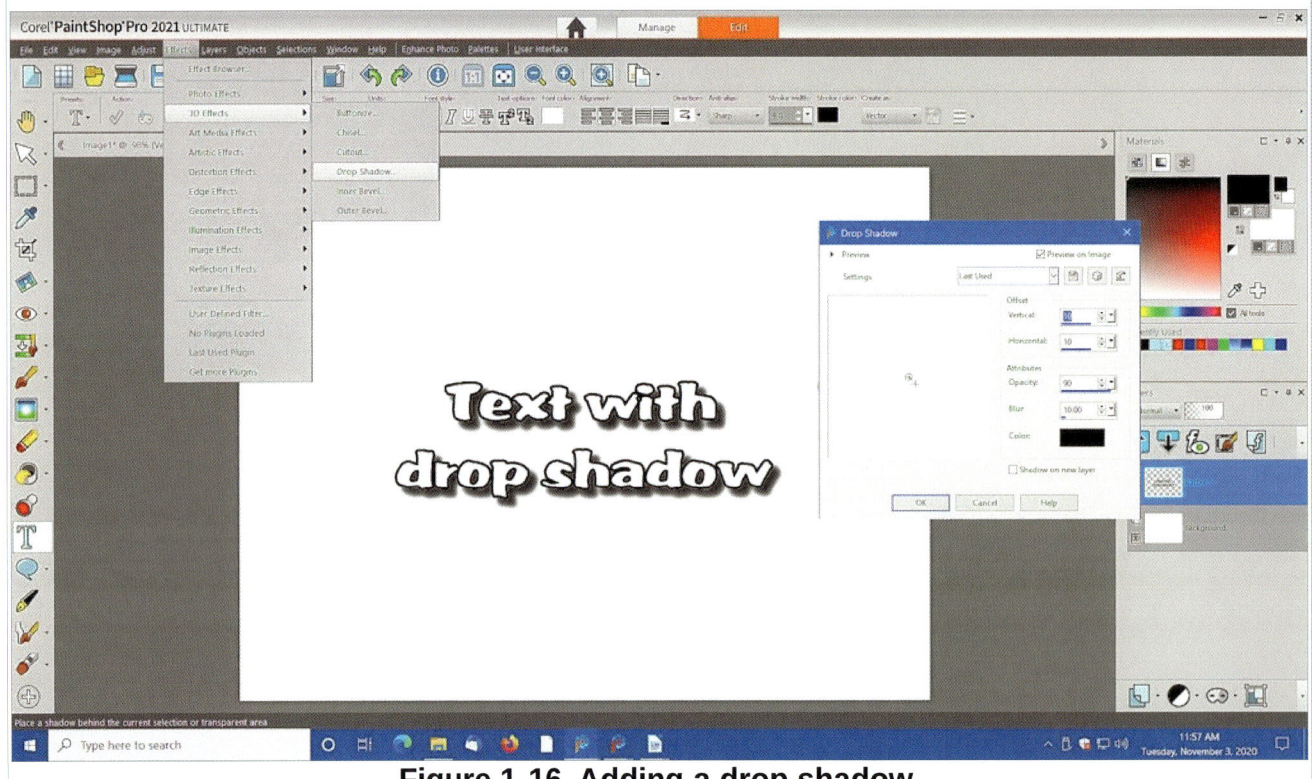

Figure 1-16, Adding a drop shadow.

- With the text box selected, from the **Menubar** select **Effects, 3D Effects, Drop shadow**.
- If necessary, convert the image to raster.
- In the **Drop Shadow** dialog box, set **Vertical** and Horizontal to **10**.
- Set **Opacity** to **90**.
- Set **Blur** to **10**. Then select **OK**.

You should add some new text and experiment with the different Drop Shadow options.

Modifying a Text Layer

- ***Close all*** Paint Shop Pro images.
- From the practice images PDF file, Select the **Figure 18, Clouds** image from the PDF file. image, *right click*, and then select **Copy Image**.
- Use the ***Taskbar*** or press ***Alt+tab*** and switch to Paint Shop Pro window.
- From the Paint Shop Pro ***Menubar***, select **Edit, Paste as New Image** [or, press **Shift+Insert**].
- Select the ***Text*** tool, set the ***Font*** to **Arial 200 Bold**.
- Set the ***Font color*** to **red** and the ***Stroke width*** to **2**.

Part 1 - Drawing

- Enter text similar to Figure 1-17.

- Use the **Pick** tool to select the text, then **center** the text horizontally and vertically.
- From the **Menubar**, select **Effects, 3D Effects, Inner Bevel**.
- Experiment with the **Inner Bevel** options until you are happy with the result, then select **OK**.

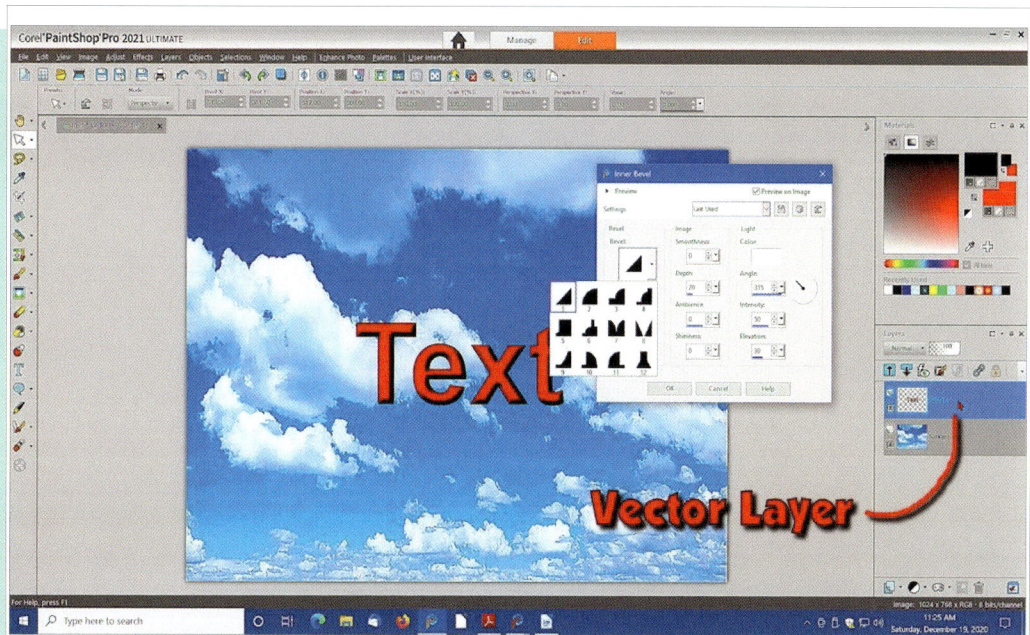

Figure 1-17: Text on clouds.

- Right click on the text and select Properties.
- In the properties dialog box **General** tab, set the **Blend Mode** to **Overlay**.
- In the properties dialog box **Layer Styles** tab, toggle the **Layer** and **Bevel** options **ON**.

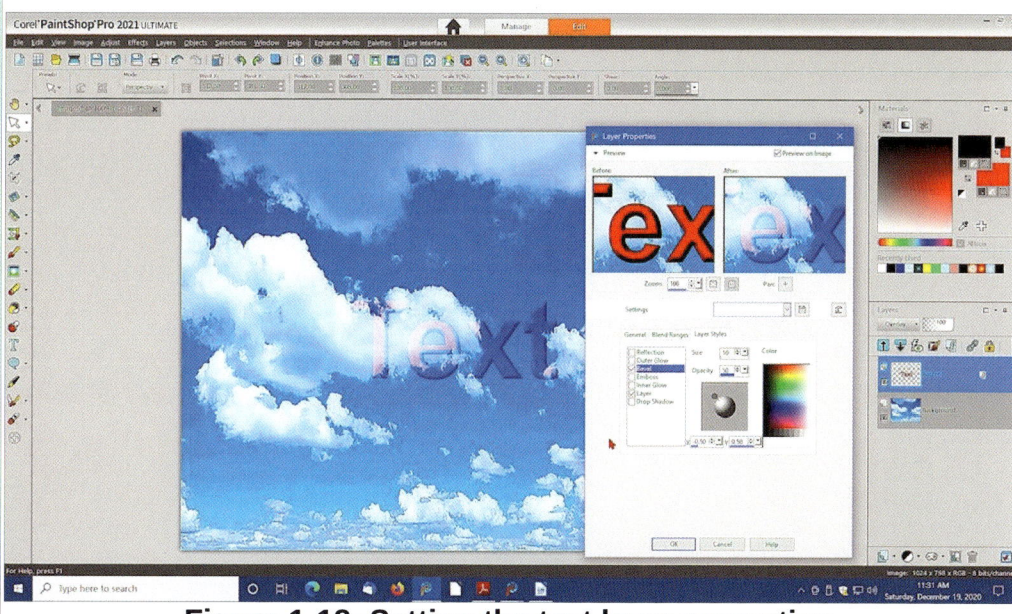

Figure 1-18: Setting the text layer properties.

Page 19

Paint Shop Pro 2021 Fundamentals

Note that when the text is selected, you can adjust perspective and shear properties.

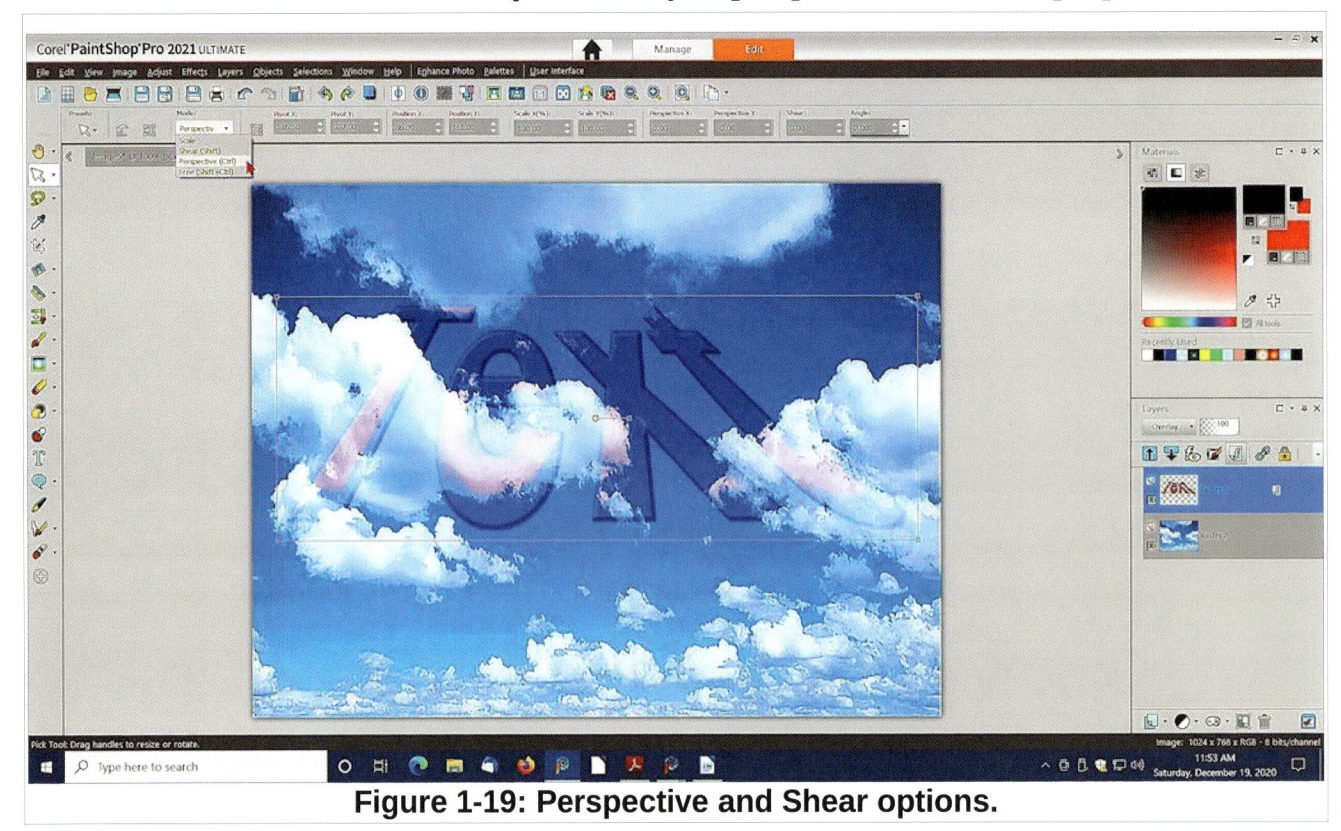

Figure 1-19: Perspective and Shear options.

Text Cutter Tool

The Text Cutter Tool Provides a way to fill the text with a part of an image. It works sort of like using a cookie cutter to cut a special shape… Think gingerbread man or heart shaped cookies.

To use the **Text Cutter**, we need to start with an existing image. In this example, I will open an image from my picture collection. Here is the process.

- ✓ Open an image file
- ✓ Add text to the open image and have the text nearly fill the display.
- ✓ Select the **Text Cutter** tool.

This will open a new image.

- ✓ Add a *drop shadow* to the new image.
- ✓ Use **Ctrl+C** to copy the new image.
- ✓ Open a new 1024x768 drawing.

- Use **Ctrl+V** to paste the copied image.

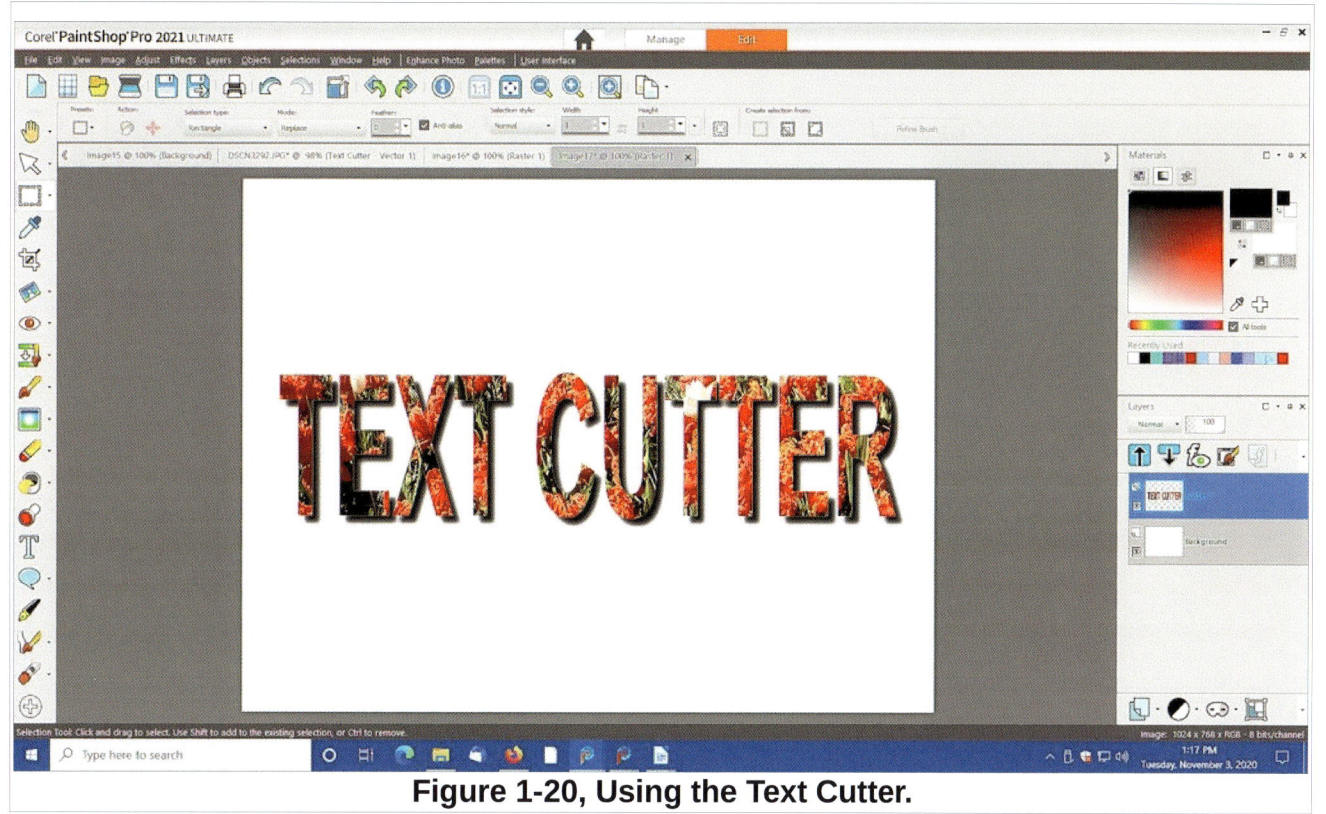

Figure 1-20, Using the Text Cutter.

The **Text Cutter** makes it easy to fill text from an image. If you save the new Text Cutter image to a file, you can add the image to other drawings, or even word processing documents or email messages.

Creating Curved Text

Paint Shop Pro allows for creating text that follows a curved line.

- Open a new 1024x768 drawing.
- Select the **Pen Tool**.
- From the **Pen Tool** options, select **Draw Freehand**.
- Add a **curved line** similar to that shown in Figure 1-21.

Paint Shop Pro 2021 Fundamentals

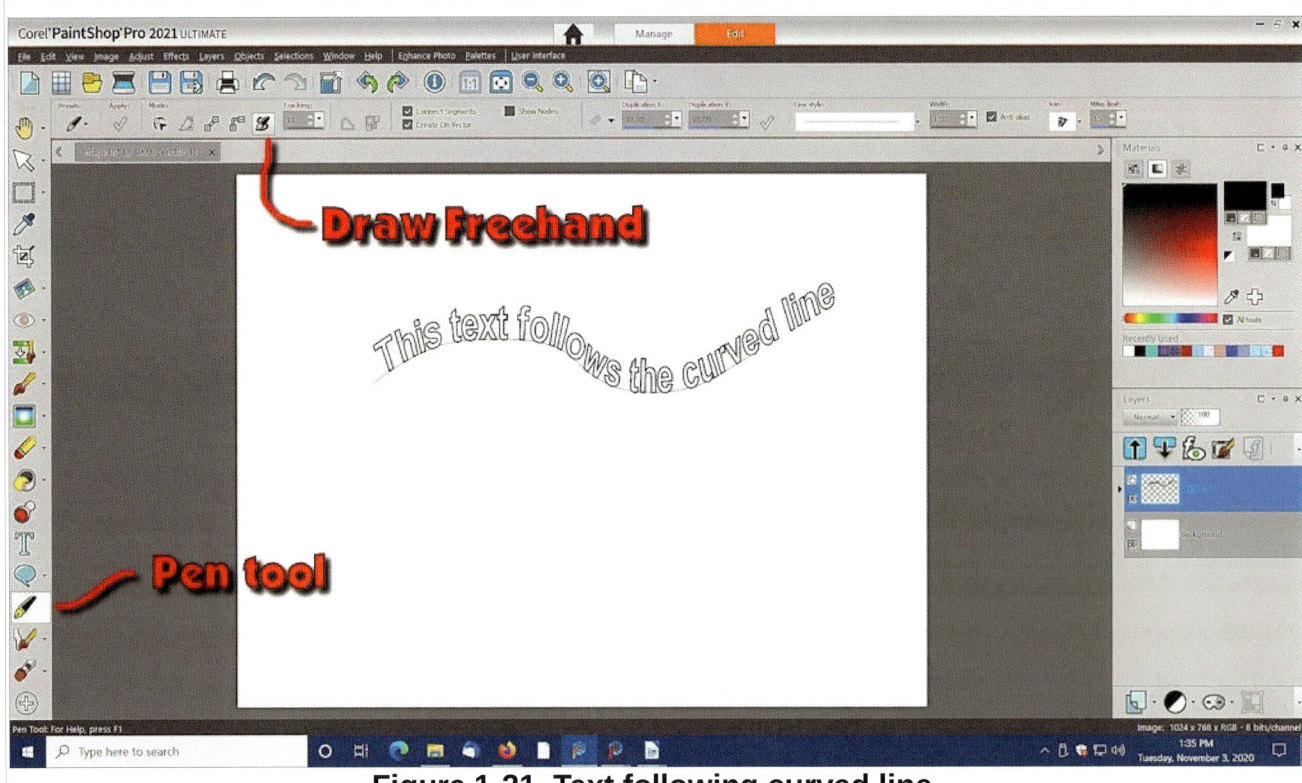

Figure 1-21, Text following curved line.

Picture Tube Fun

Picture tubes are a fun way to quickly create drawings. Be sure you have installed the Paint Shop Pro Creative Collection.

> The **Creative Collection** is a set of brushes, textures, frames, lines styles, mask, preset shapes. They can be found on the Picture tube Menu, Texture menu, and Picture frame menu.
>
> If you do not have PSP 2021 Ultimate, you may be able to find the creative collection on earlier versions of PSP. I have seen PSP X9 Ultimate for as low as $16. Look for new (not used) versions of Paint Shop Pro Ultimate X4 or newer.
>
> Go to the **Store** on the **Welcome** screen, check the Creative Content *filter* option, scroll down and install the Free **Creative Content** and **Brush Pack**.

✓ Open a new 1024x768 drawing.

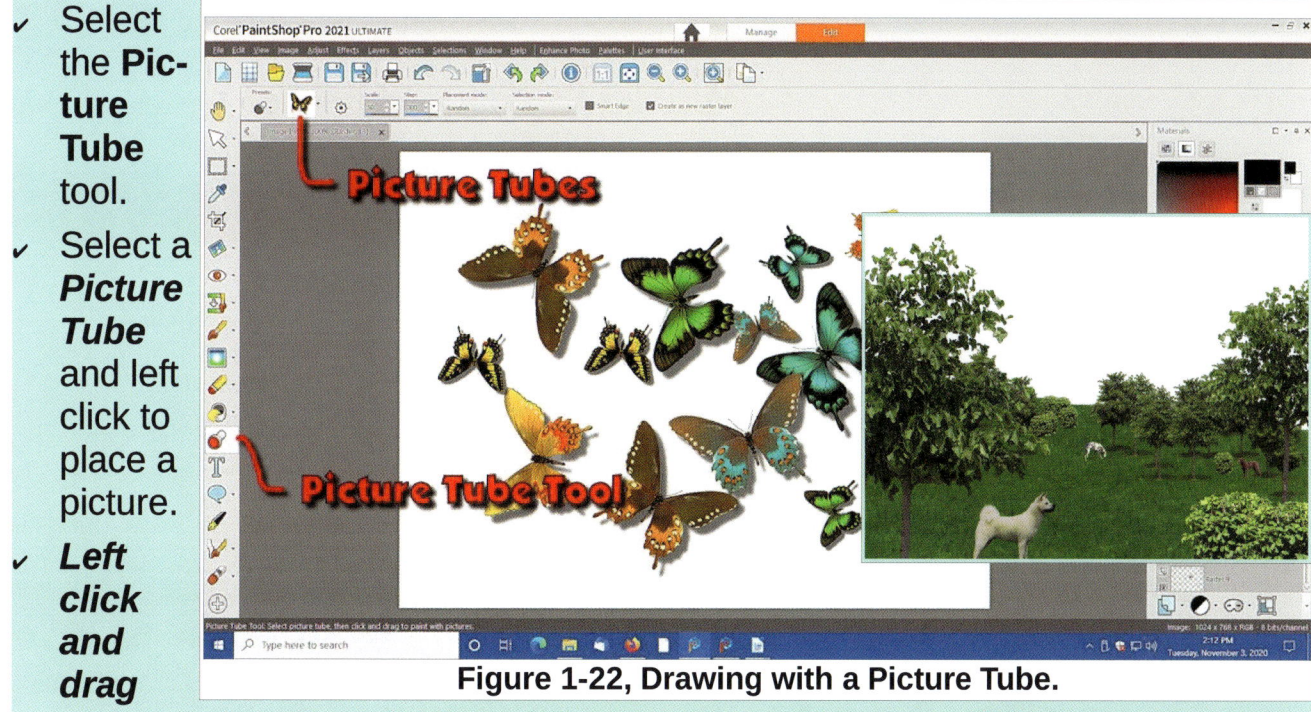

Part 1 - Drawing

- ✓ Select the **Picture Tube** tool.
- ✓ Select a **Picture Tube** and left click to place a picture.
- ✓ **Left click and drag** and note the effect. (Different Picture Tubes will function differently when using click and drag.)
- ✓ Experiment with different **Picture Tubes**.

Figure 1-22, Drawing with a Picture Tube.

The Flood Fill Tool

- ✓ Open a new 1024x768 drawing.
- ✓ Choose different colors for the *foreground* and *background*.
- ✓ Select the **Flood Fill** tool.
- ✓ Select a color and then select an empty section of the display and press the *left* mouse button.
- ✓ Select **Undo**, and then fill using the *right* mouse button.

You can flood fill with either the foreground or background color.

The **Flood Full *Context Toolbar*** provides options to change the flood fill properties.

You should also explore using flood fill with gradient, patterns, or textures instead of solid colors

Paint Shop Pro 2021 Fundamentals

Before and After Enhancing

Page 24

Part 2 – Enhancing Photos

Enhancing Photos

A common use of Paint Shop Pro 2021 is enhancing digital photos. A few tricks for improving pictures are presented in this section. In order to import images for practice, the next steps will show how to copy an image from a document and paste it as a new image in Paint Shop Pro.

The practice images are available in a PDF file online. Go to the following web page address on the Internet, select the **Paint Shop Pro 2021** tab, then select the **Sample Image Book** download option.

http://lenshamn.com/learnatlenshamn.html

- From the practice images PDF file, Select the **Figure 3, Fall Grass** image from the PDF file. image, *right click*, and then select **Copy Image**.
- Use the *Taskbar* or press *Alt+tab* and switch to Paint Shop Pro window.
- From the Paint Shop Pro *Menubar*, select **Edit, Paste as New Image** [or, press **Shift+Insert**].

Once the image is open, it will appear in Paint Shop Pro with a tab. It is possible to have a number of different image windows open at the same time. These will either appear as separate windows or as tabs.

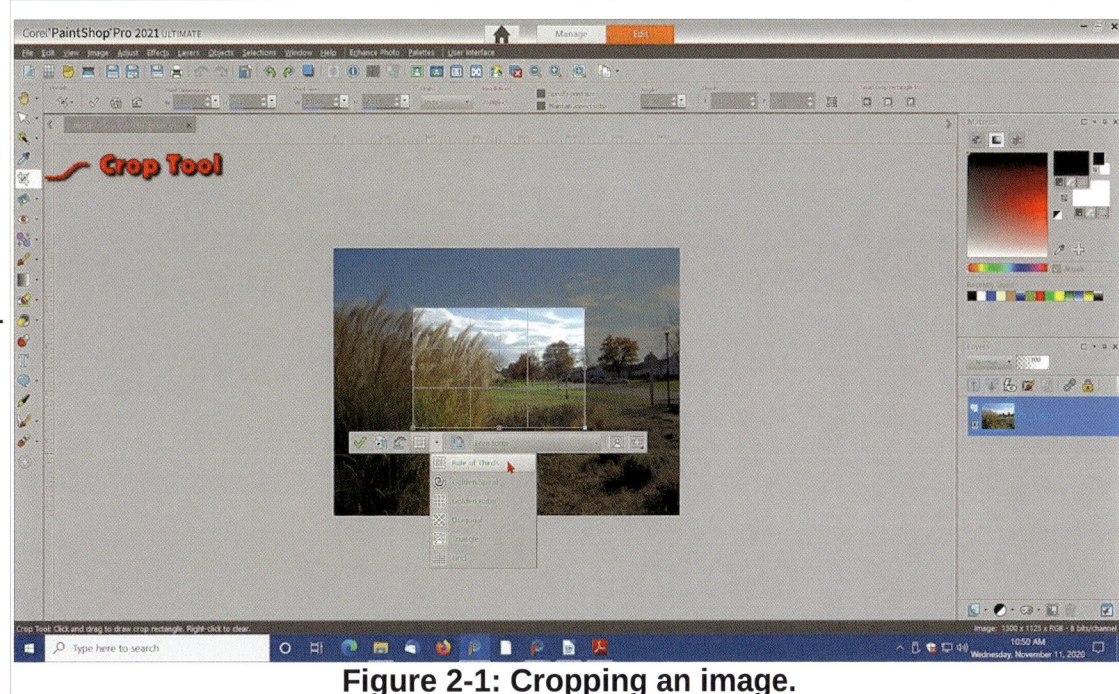

Figure 2-1: Cropping an image.

Page 25

Paint Shop Pro 2021 Fundamentals

Cropping Images

Select the **Crop Tool** (see Figure 2-1).

The **Crop Tool** has its own tool bar (see Figure 2-2). You can **click and drag** a new crop area. If necessary, use the **Clear** option to remove any existing cropping area.

Once a cropping area has been defined, you can either select the **Apply** tool to change the existing image, or use the **Crop to New Image** tool to create a new image from the cropping area.

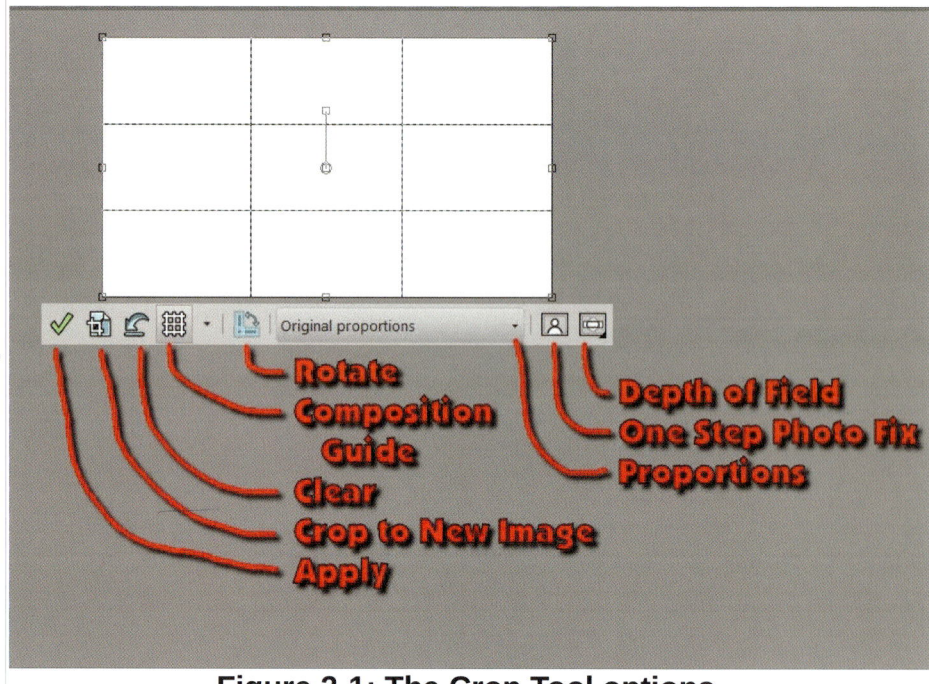

Figure 2-1: The Crop Tool options.

Since the days of the 'Old Masters', artists have used several composition styles to improve their work. The **Composition Guide** provides cropping options that follow established '**rules of thumb**' for artistic compositions.

If you are interested in composition rules, do an internet search on any of the Paint Shop Pro composition style options, or search for *image composition rules*.

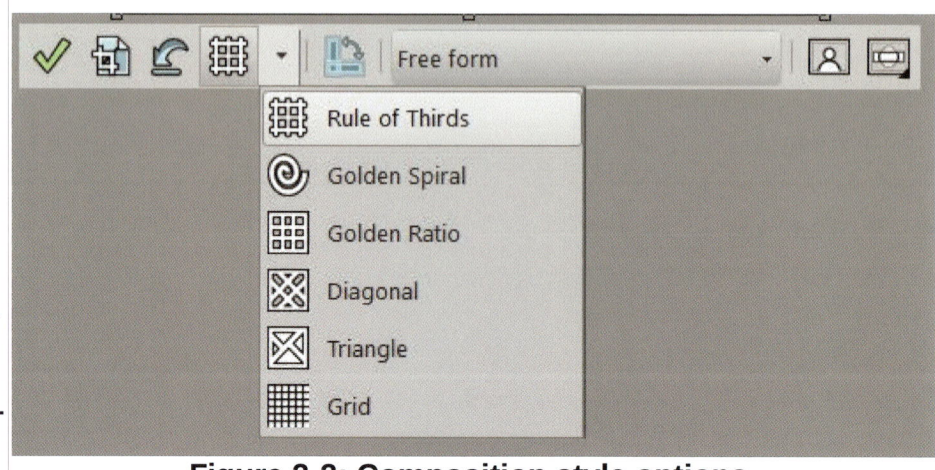

Figure 2-2: Composition style options.

Part 2 – Enhancing Photos

The **Proportions** options provide for standard aspect ratios commonly used for printing images.

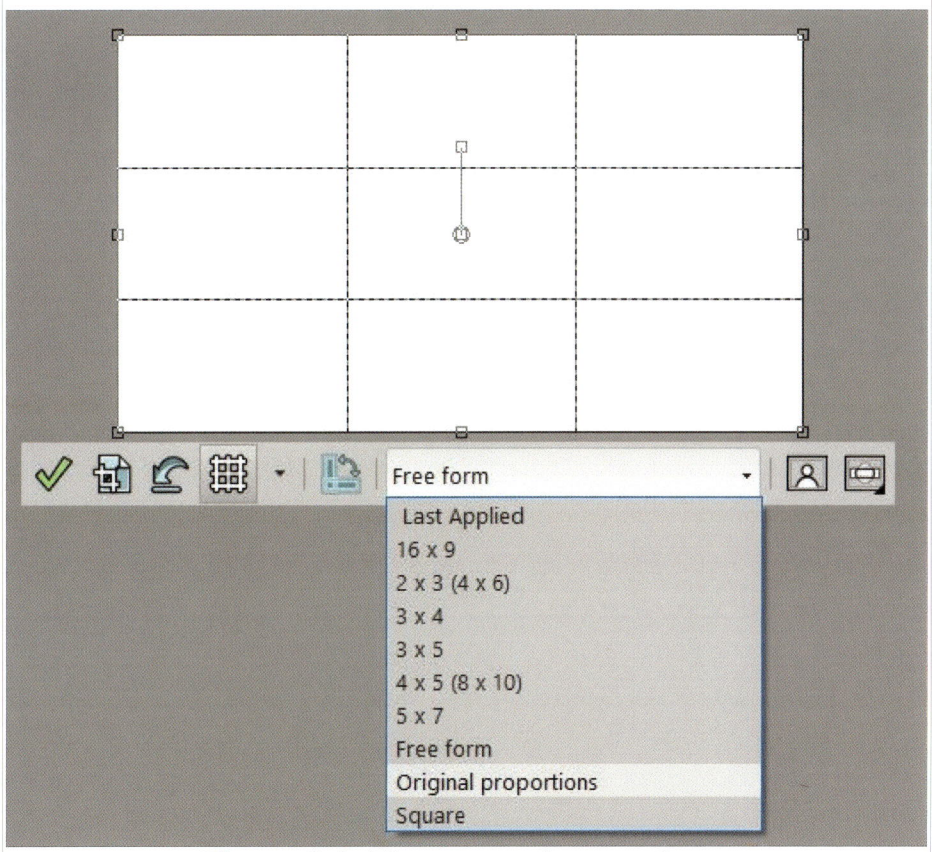

Figure 2-3: The proportions options.

Observe that except for the **Free Form** proportions option, when the **grab points** for a cropping selection are dragged, the proportions remain fixed.

Figure 2-4: Cropping grab points.

Paint Shop Pro 2021 Fundamentals

- Use the **Figure 3, Fall Grass** image to practice using the **Crop Tool**.
- Use the **Clear** tool (in the cropping tool area) to drag a new crop area.
- Use the **Crop As New Image** tool to create a new picture that uses the current crop area. (Use the **File, Save As** tool to rename and save the new image.)

Note that the **Crop As New Image** option has added a **new tab** to the Paint Shop Pro display.

When more than one image is open at the same time in Paint Shop Pro, there are several ways that the image windows can be displayed. In Figure 2-6, the **Tabs** option is being used.

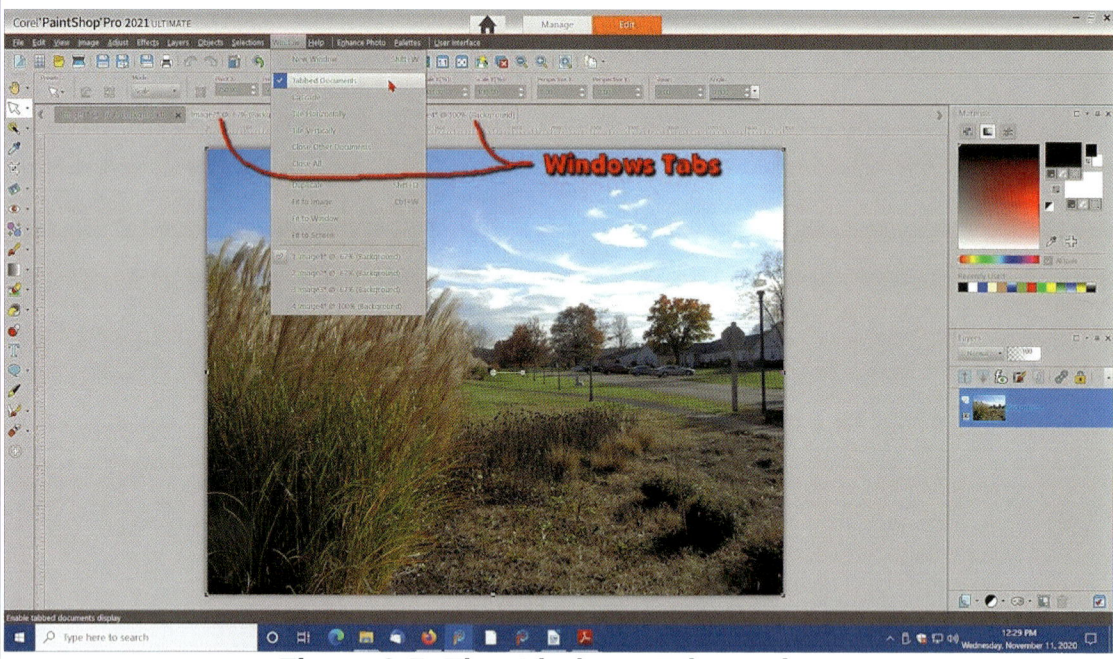

Figure 2-5: The Windows Tabs option.

If you use the **Crop As New Image** option it is easy to compare the different images by selecting an image tab. Figure 2-7 shows multiple image windows open and resized to compare different image cropping results.

- Use the Fall Grass image to experiment with the different cropping options.
- Use the Crop As New Image option to cre-

Figure 2-6: Multiple image windows.

Page 28

Part 2 – Enhancing Photos

ate new images and then experiment with the different windows display options.

If you ever want to see your new images again, be sure to use **File, Save As**, and save a copy of your images in a known location for later use.

Adding Picture Frames

Paint Shop Pro provides a number of different picture frames that can be used to enhance your images.

The **Creative Collection** is a set of brushes, textures, **frames**, lines styles, mask, preset shapes. They can be found on the Picture tube Menu, Texture menu, and **Picture frame menu**.

If you do not have PSP 2021 Ultimate, you may be able to find the creative collection on earlier versions of PSP. I have seen PSP X9 Ultimate for as low as $16. Look for new (not used) versions of Paint Shop Pro Ultimate X4 or newer.

✓ Open one of your favorite images.

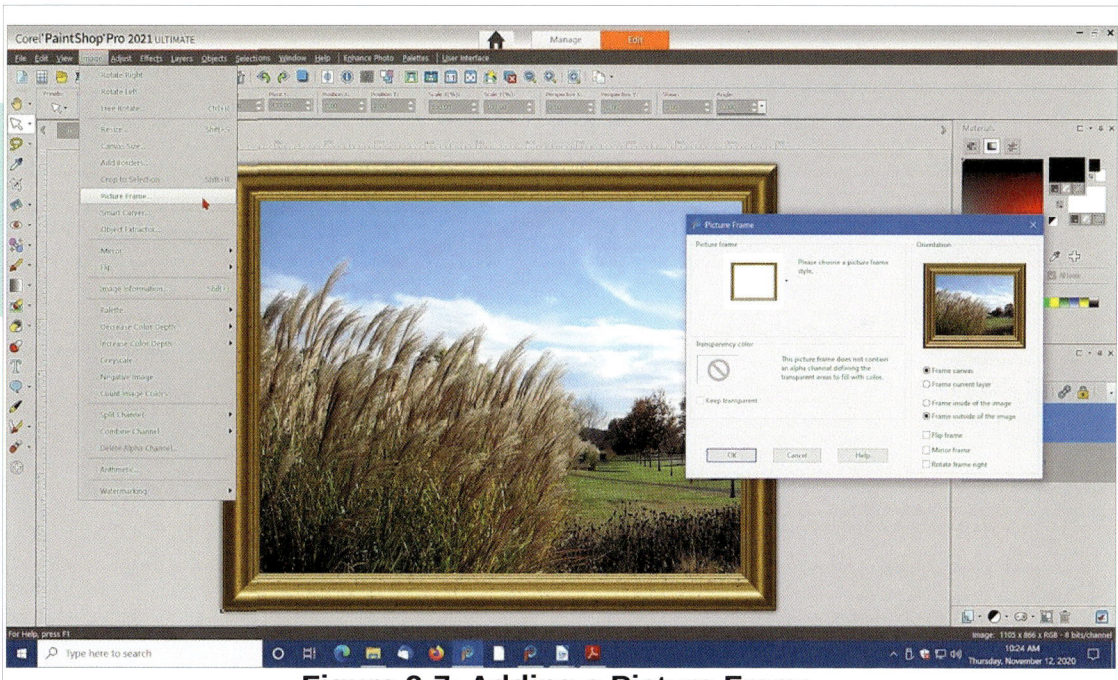

Figure 2-7: Adding a Picture Frame.

✓ From the *Menubar*, select **Image, Picture Frame**.
✓ Select a picture frame for your image.

Page 29

Paint Shop Pro 2021 Fundamentals

Straighten and Perspective Correction Tools

There are times when you have a photograph where the horizon seems to run down hill. This issue is typically most noticeable when a scene includes a lake or ocean. However, it can also happen in normal pictures as well.

If you take a picture where the axis of camera lens was not pointed perpendicular to an object in the picture, there will be perspective distortion. Paint Shop Pro has tools to deal with both slanted horizon and perspective distortion situations.

- Open the **Figure 4,Fall Street image** from the practice images PDF file.
- **Select** the image, **right click** and select **Copy**, then paste the copy as a new image in Paint Shop Pro.
- Select the **Straighten Tool** and create a new horizon line as shown in Figure 2-9,
- Select **Apply** from the **Toolbar**.

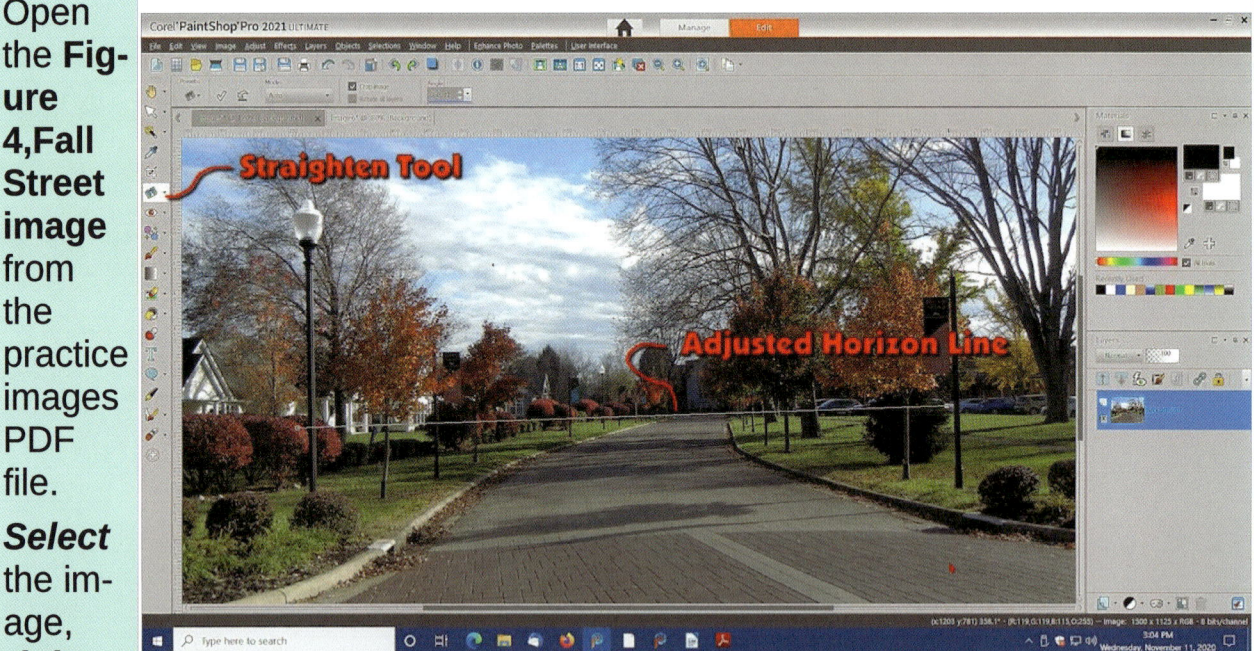

Figure 2-8: Using the Straighten Tool.

Now that the horizon has been adjusted, experiment with different croppings of this image.

Next, the perspective correction tool will be explored.

Part 2 – Enhancing Photos

- Open the **Figure 2, Display Case 2** from the practice images PDF file.
- **Select** the image, **right click** and select **Copy**, then paste the copy as a new image in Paint Shop Pro.
- Select the **Perspective Correction Tool** and drag the corners of the correction box as shown in Figure 2-10,
- Select **Apply** from the **Toolbar**.

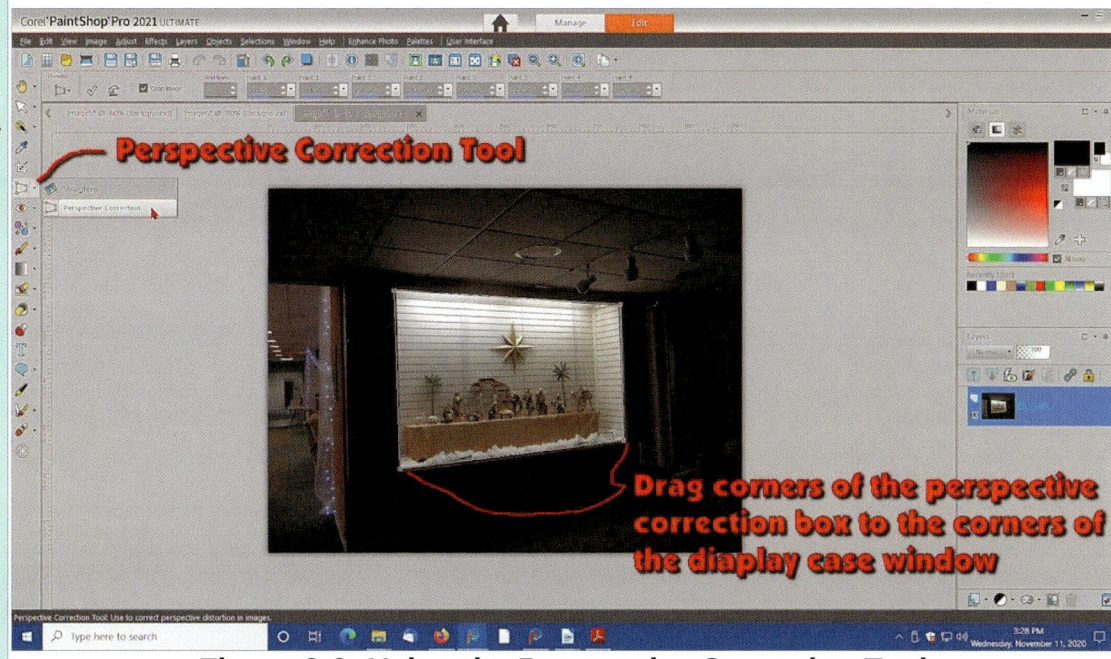

Figure 2-9: Using the Perspective Correction Tool.

Just like magic, the system fixes the perspective problem. Now you can crop the corrected image.

Figure 2-10: Corrected perspective.

Resizing Images

New digital cameras, even many in the under US $100 class, can create high resolution images. For example the original image in Figure 2-11 was taken with a 12 megapixel camera and the original image was 4000 by 3000 pixels in size.

If you are adding images to word processing documents, web pages, or if you are emailing images, a 4000 pixel image is overkill, will have an unnecessarily large file size, and result in slow email transmission times.

Most of the sample images included in this document were reduced to a width of 1024 pixels to keep the file size of this document manageable. Paint Shop Pro 2021 makes it easy to resize your pictures to a manageable file size.

- With the **Fall Street** image on the display (as seen in Figure 2-11), observe the image size in the info area.
- Select the **Resize** tool.

This opens the **Resize** dialog box. The **By Pixels** option will be used in this exercise. Also toggle the **Advanced Settings** and **Lock aspect ratio** options **ON**.

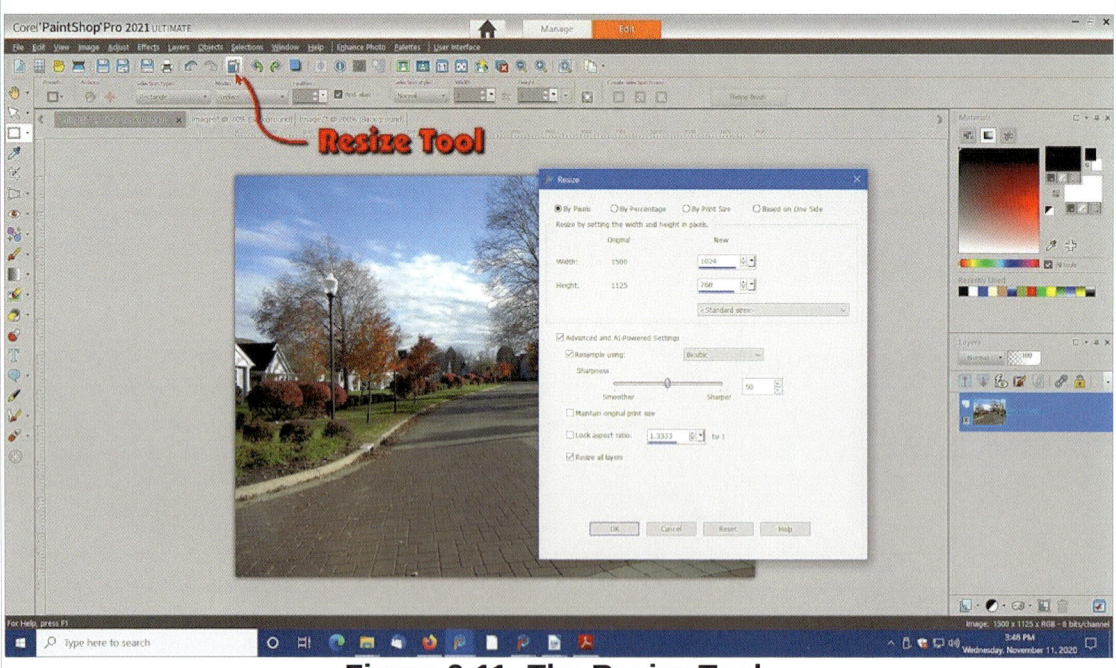

Figure 2-11: The Resize Tool.

If you wanted to email this image to a friend without filling the mail box or taking too long to transmit, a width of 600 pixels will be adequate. It is possible to change the aspect ratio during resizing an image. Typically, the aspect ratio should be locked on.

- Toggle the **By Pixels** option **ON**.
- Make sure there is a check beside the **Lock aspect ratio**.
- Set the new width to **600** and then select **OK**.

Changing image pixel width has a dramatic effect on image file size. The file size of the 4000 ×3000 version of the picture shown was 2,615 KB, while the 1024 pixel wide version was 272 KB. The 600 pixel wide version file size is 107KB. A 600 resolution image attached to an email will look very good. Images of 1024 can be printed up to 8 × 10 inches with good results.

The only times I need image resolutions of 4000 pixels or more is when I want to print a very large poster or if I want to crop a small area out of an image and still have a presentable quality image. I have created a large collection of my photos to use as wallpaper for the computer desktop, or for screen saver images. Since my monitor has a resolution of 1920x1080 I resize photos to that dimension.

Whenever you want to reduce file size of images use the Paint Shop Pro *resize* tool. You can also increase the size of an image and at the same time smooth out the pixelation.

- ✔ Open the **Figure 14, Family 8 image** from the practice images PDF file.
- ✔ *Select* the image, *right click* and select *Copy*, then paste the copy as a new image in Paint Shop Pro.

You should remember how to fix the slanted horizon.

After the horizon issue is fixed the image can be improved by dropping.

Figure 2-12: Adjusting the horizon.

- ✔ Select the **Straighten** tool and adjust the horizon.
- ✔ **Crop** the image to improve the picture.

This picture started with a low resolution, and after cropping the resolution was even smaller. If you zoom in on the image, you will see the individual pixels that make up the image.

Paint Shop Pro 2021 Fundamentals

If the image size is increased, the pixel size will also increase. The good news is that Paint Shop Pro 2021 has a way to increase resolution while decreasing the size of the pixels.

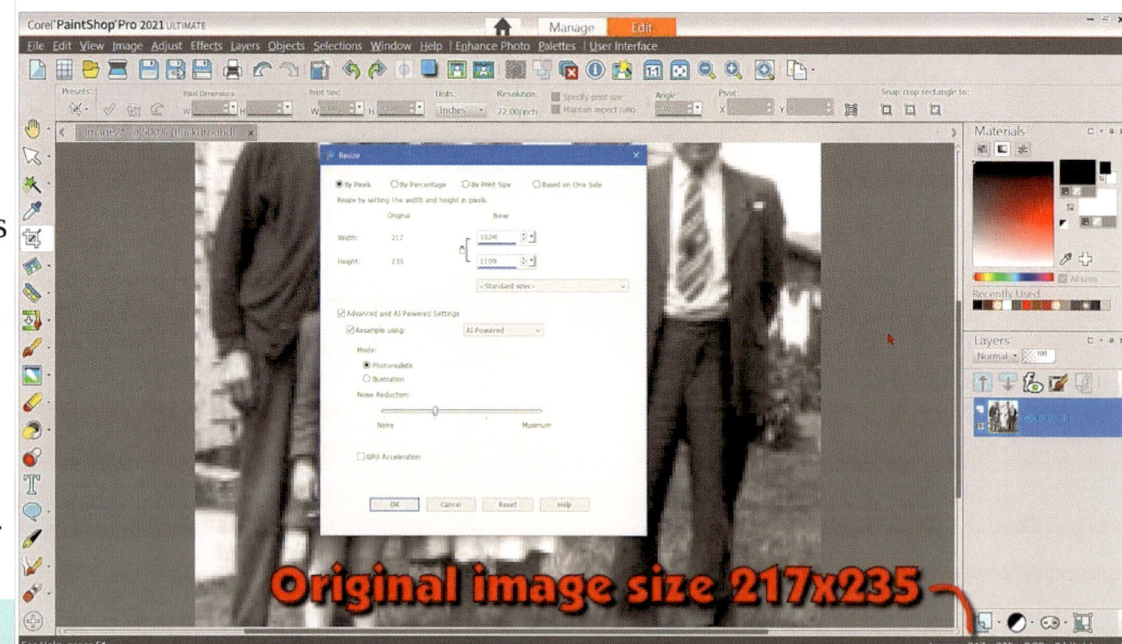

Figure 2-13: Cropped Family 8 picture.

- With the cropped Family 8 image open, from the *Menubar* select **Image, Resize**.
- In the *Resize* dialog box toggle the **Advanced and AI Powered Settings** ON.
- Set the new pixel width to **1024** and select **OK**.

The resizing function calculations take a little time to complete. The AI magic has improved the resolution of the picture. You can see this if you zoom in on the before and after versions.

Figure 2-14: Resolution improvement.

Page 34

Part 2 – Enhancing Photos

Enhancing Images

- With the **Fall Street** image on the display, observe the color balance of the image.
- From the **Menubar** select **Enhance Photo, One Step Photo Fix**.
- Select **Undo** and **Redo** a couple of times to observe the changes.
- The **One Step Photo Fix** tool is an easy way to improve images.

A more advanced than the One Step Photo Fix is the **Smart Photo Fix** tool. The **Smart Photo Fix** tool provides sliders that allow adjustments while observing the effects of the adjustments.

- Open the **Figure 15, Scan 2** image from the practice images PDF file.
- **Select** the image, **right click** and select **Copy**, then paste the copy as a new image in Paint Shop Pro.
- From the **Menubar** select **Enhance Photo, Smart Photo Fix**.

Figure 2-12 shows the **One Step Photo Fix** tool being used on **Figure 15, Scan 2** from the practice images PDF file.

Figure 2-15: Using Smart Photo Fix on an old photo.

- Experiment with the different adjustment options in the **Smart Photo Fix** dialog box.
- When you are satisfied with the changes, select **OK**.

Page 35

Paint Shop Pro 2021 Fundamentals

Additional improvements can be made to this photo by changing to a greyscale image and then using the Brightness and Contrast tools.

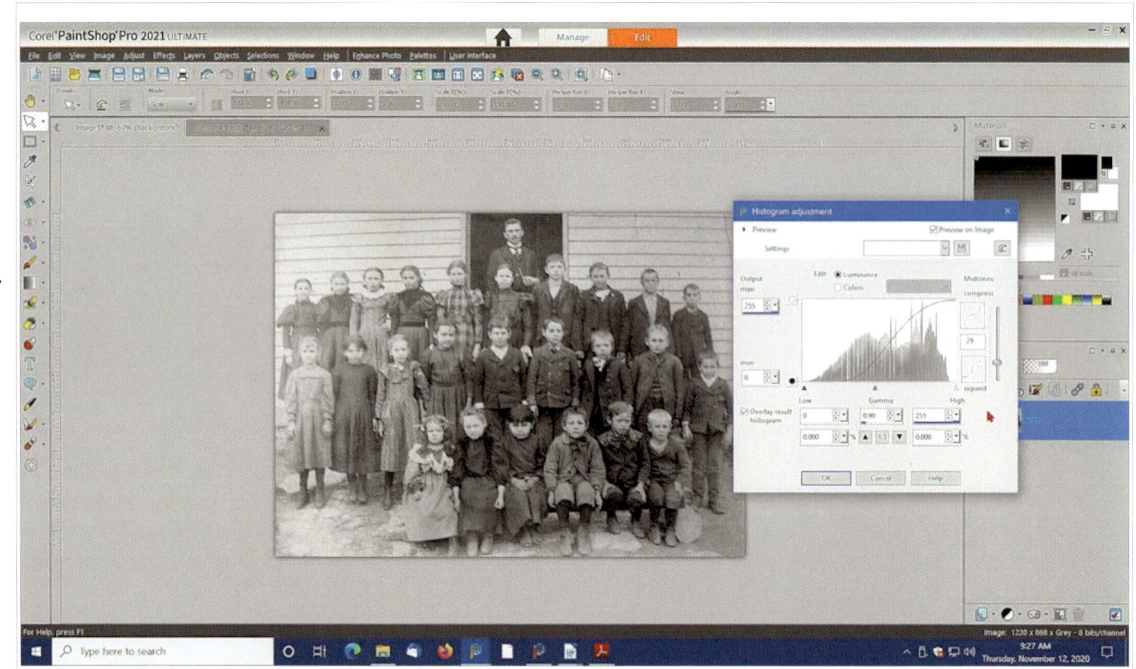

Adjusting Brightness and Contrast

- With the modified **Figure 15, Scan 2** image open, select **File Save As**, select a folder for your practice images, and then enter **Class Photo** as the file name.
- From the **Menubar** select **Image, Greyscale**.
- From the **Menubar**, select **Adjust, Brightness and Contrast, Histogram Adjustment**.
- Make sure that the **Preview on image** option is toggles **ON**.
- Experiment with the **Gamma** and **Midtone** sliders until you have an image you like.

Figure 2-16 shows Brightness and Contrast adjustments. I know of no 'rule of thumb' for settings to use. However, experimenting with the settings enables you to quickly get good results.

Figure 2-16: Adjusting Brightness and Contrast.

You probably have noticed that the left side of the photo is lighter than the right side. There is a trick that can be used to minimize this lighting unbalance problem. The trick is to use a selection tool to capture the area to change, and then apply Brightness and Contrast adjustments to the selected area.

Part 2 – Enhancing Photos

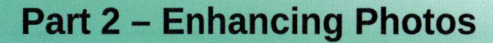

- From the **Toolbar**, select the Freehand Selection tool.
- Capture the area to adjust, and use the Brightness and Contrast tool to improve the selection.

Figure 2-17 shows a selection with the Brightness and Contrast exaggerated to more clearly show the selected area.

- When you are satisfied with your adjustments to the selected area, from the **Menubar** select **Selections, Select None**.

Figure 2-17: Selecting an area.

With a little work, you can take an old faded scanned photo and improve it considerably. It is, in some cases, possible to restore photos that are almost impossible to view otherwise. Figure 2-18 shows before and after versions of the **Figure 12, Family 6** image from the practice images PDF file.

Figure 2-18: Before and after adjustments.

The Vibrancy Tool

Another tool that can make your images a little more dramatic is the **Vibrancy** tool.

- From the practice images PDF file, Select the **Figure 3, Fall Trees** image from the PDF file. image, *right click*, and then select **Copy Image**.

Paint Shop Pro 2021 Fundamentals

- Use the **Taskbar** or press **Alt+tab** and switch to Paint Shop Pro window.
- From the Paint Shop Pro **Menubar**, select **Edit, Paste as New Image** [or, press **Shift+Insert**].
- From the **Menubar**, select **Adjust, Hue and Saturation, Vibrancy**.
- Experiment with the **Strength** slider and observe the results.

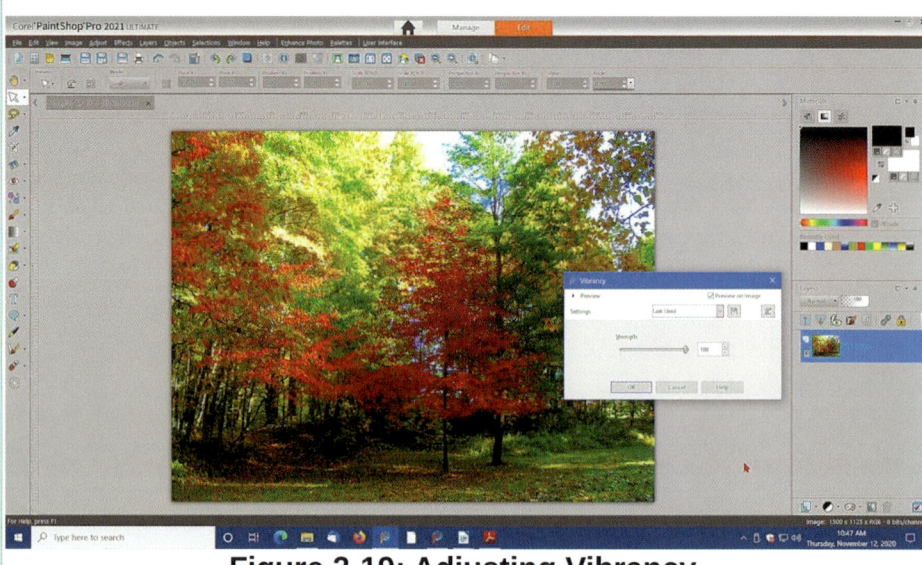

Figure 2-19: Adjusting Vibrancy.

Applying **Vibrancy** to images can make for more dramatic pictures. Especially when the pictures include fall leaves.

Figure 2-20: Applying Vibrancy.

One Step Noise Removal

The One Step Noise Removal tool can be used to smooth out some scanned images.

- From the practice images PDF file, Select the **Figure 14, Scan 1** image from the PDF file. image, *right click*, and then select **Copy Image**.
- Use the **Taskbar** or press **Alt+tab** and switch to Paint Shop Pro window.

Part 2 – Enhancing Photos

- From the Paint Shop Pro *Menubar*, select **Edit, Paste as New Image** [or, press **Shift+Insert**].
- From the *Menubar*, select **One Step Noise Removal** tool.

This image was scanned from an old newspaper, and the One Step Noise Removal tool can smooth out the image a little bit.

Figure 2-21: The One Step Noise Removal tool.

- After applying the **One Step Noise Removal tool**, switch between **Undo** and **Redo** to observe the change to the image.

The Lighten/Darken tool

A little cropping can improve the picture. Also, removing distracting background can be accomplished by using the **Lighten/ Darken tool**. The same tool

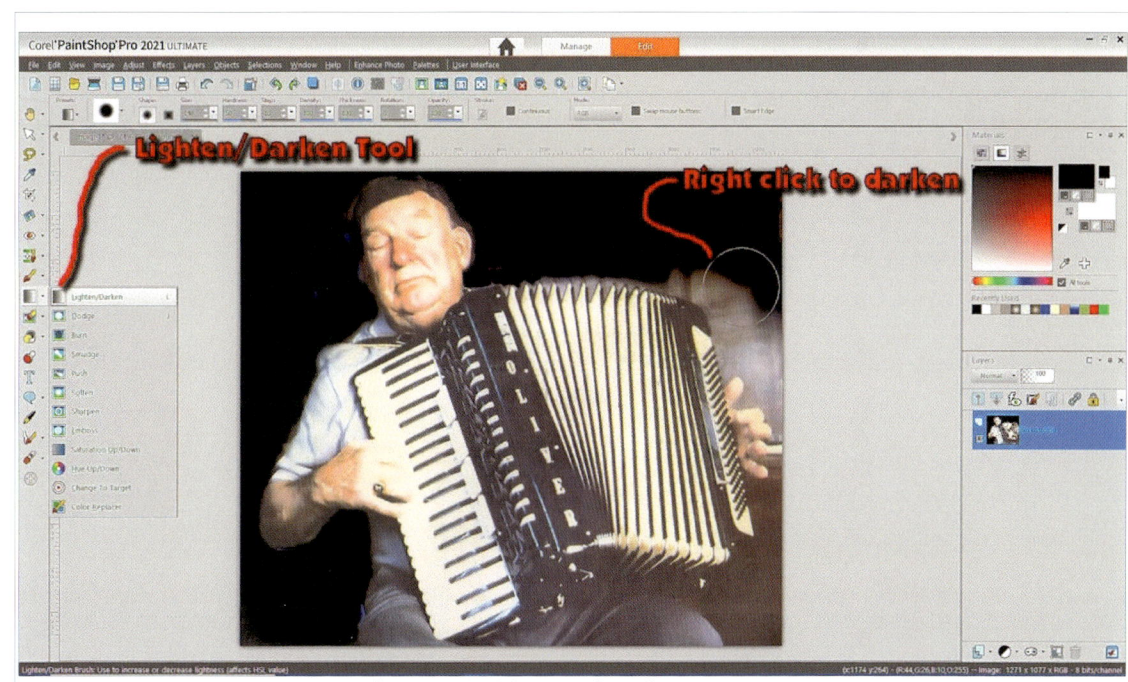

Figure 2-22: Darkening areas.

Page 39

is used for both to lighten and darken areas of an image. Left click to lighten and right click to darken.

✓ Use the **Lighten/Darken** tool to black out unwanted areas of the picture.

Blacking out as much as seen in Figure 2-24, requires a lot of zooming in and out and changing the brush size. It's a time consuming process.

Figure 2-23: Before and after darkening background.

It is not unusual for old pictures to contain spots and scratches. These problems can be fixed using **Paint Shop Pro 2021**.

The Scratch Remover Tool

✓ From the practice images PDF file, Select the **Figure 7, Fam-**

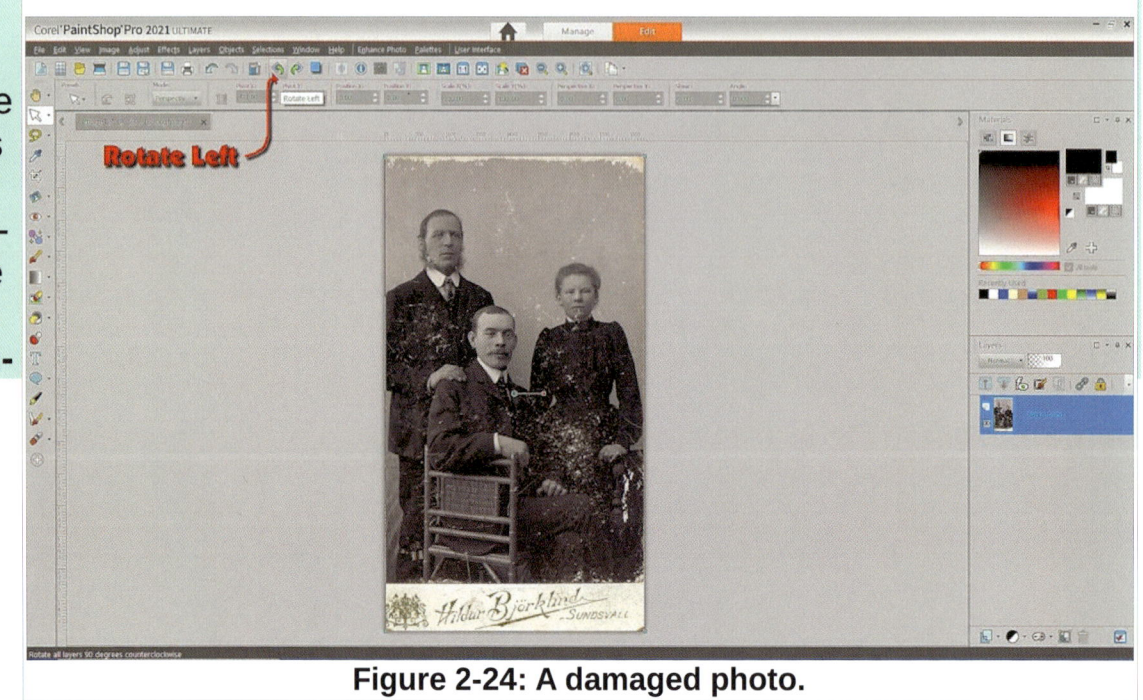

Figure 2-24: A damaged photo.

Page 40

Part 2 – Enhancing Photos

- **ily 1** image from the PDF file. image, *right click*, and then select **Copy Image**.
- Use the *Taskbar* or press *Alt+tab* and switch to Paint Shop Pro window.
- From the Paint Shop Pro *Menubar*, select **Edit, Paste as New Image** [or, press **Shift+Insert**].
- From the *Menubar*, select the **Rotate Left** tool.
- Use the *Cropping Tool* to capture **Aunt Selma** as shown in Figure 2-26.
- Select **Crop As New** Image.
- Switch to the new image, select *File, Save As*, and enter **Aunt Selma** as the file name.

The challenge now is to repair the damage to the photo. Both the Scratch Remover and Clone tools will be used.

With the Aunt Selma image open select the Scratch Remover tool.

To use the **Scratch Remover** tool, *left click and hold the mouse button down* at the starting point, then *drag to the ending point and release*.

Figure 25: Capturing Aunt Selma.

Observe that the Scratch Remover tool has three sections. The way it works is that pixels in the two side areas are used to replace pixels in the center area. The Scratch Remover context tools include rectangular and triangular selection options, and also a width control. When the rectangular selection option is in use, the ends if the rectangle will be perpendicular to the drag direction.

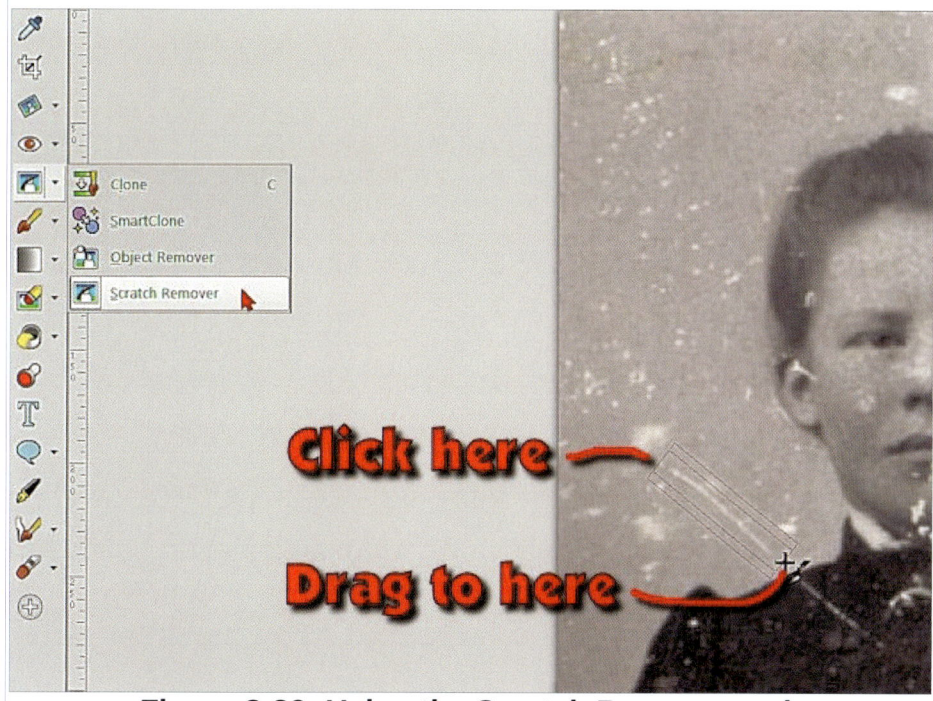

Figure 2-26: Using the Scratch Remover tool.

Page 41

Paint Shop Pro 2021 Fundamentals

> ✓ Use the **Scratch Remover** tool to remove scratches from the Aunt Selma image.

HINT: When you are dragging a scratch remover line, the width can be changed by pressing the **Page Up** or **Page Down** keys.

A tool similar to Scratch Remover, but with a radial pattern instead of a line pattern is the **Makeover, Blemish Fixer**. Give it a try on Aunt Selma.

The Scratch Remover tool will also work on spots and blemishes, However, the **Clone tool** is better for many ares.

To set the **Clone** tool, first adjust the **size** (from the Context toolbar) **Right click on an area to capture**, then drag to an area to replace.

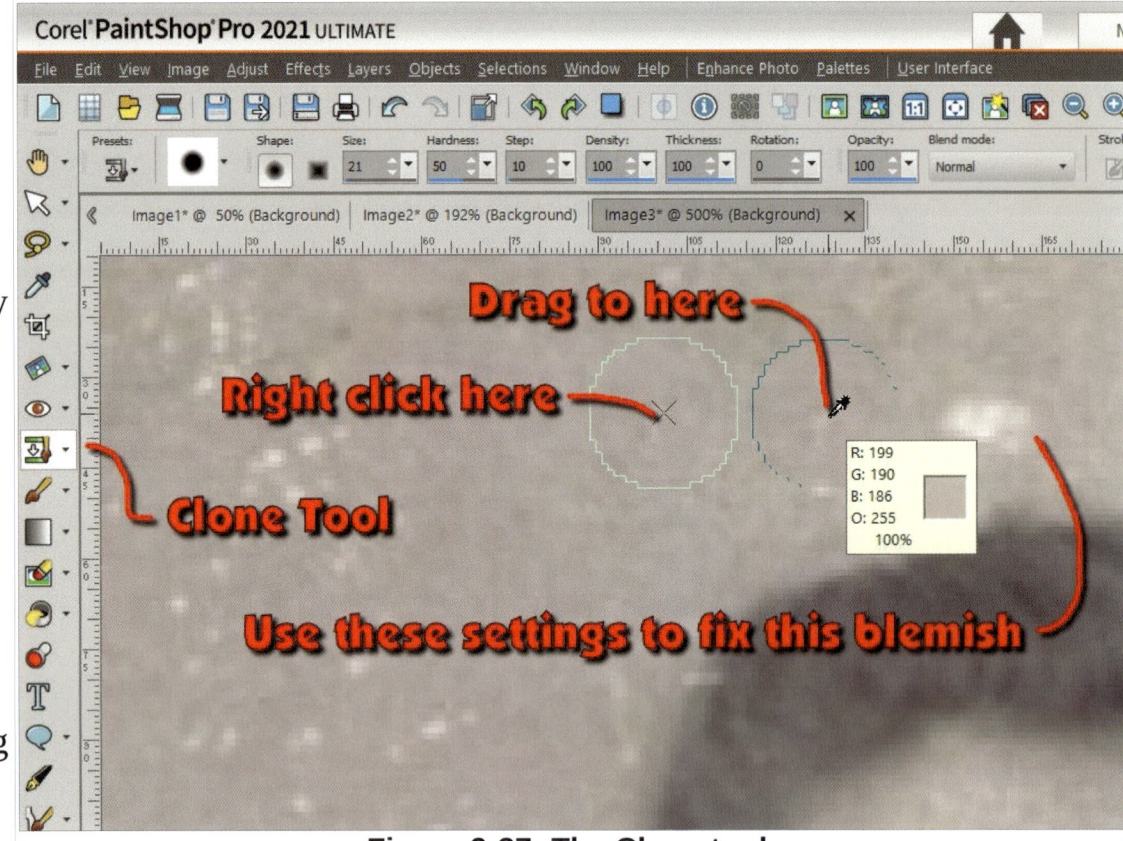

Figure 2-27: The Clone tool.

The distance and direction between the capture area and the replace area will remain constant until a new lone area is set.

> ✓ Use the **Clone** tool to repair spots and blemishes.
> ✓ Select **File, Save As** and save the image as **Aunt Selma 2**.

You will frequently have to reset the clone tool as you work over different areas of the photo. Zooming in and out will help focus on different spots.

Hint: You can change the **size** of the **Clone** tool by holding the **Alt key down** and dragging the mouse cursor.

Figure 2-28: Improved Selma.

Page 42

Part 2 – Enhancing Photos

Cleaning up old photos can require a lot of patience and take quite a bit of time. However, the results can be worth the effort.

Th Background Eraser tool.

Now that the photo of Aunt Selma has been cleaned up, we can change the background. First the current background should be removed. You could paint around the picture, but the Background Eraser tool will make this job easier.

✓ With the **Aunt Selma 2** image open, select the **Background Eraser** tool.

When you click the **Background Eraser**, the system will erase an area until it runs into pixels of a significantly different color. The Background Eraser **toolbar** provides for changing the size of the tool and other settings. You probably should review these settings and experiment with them before you start to work seriously on the photo.

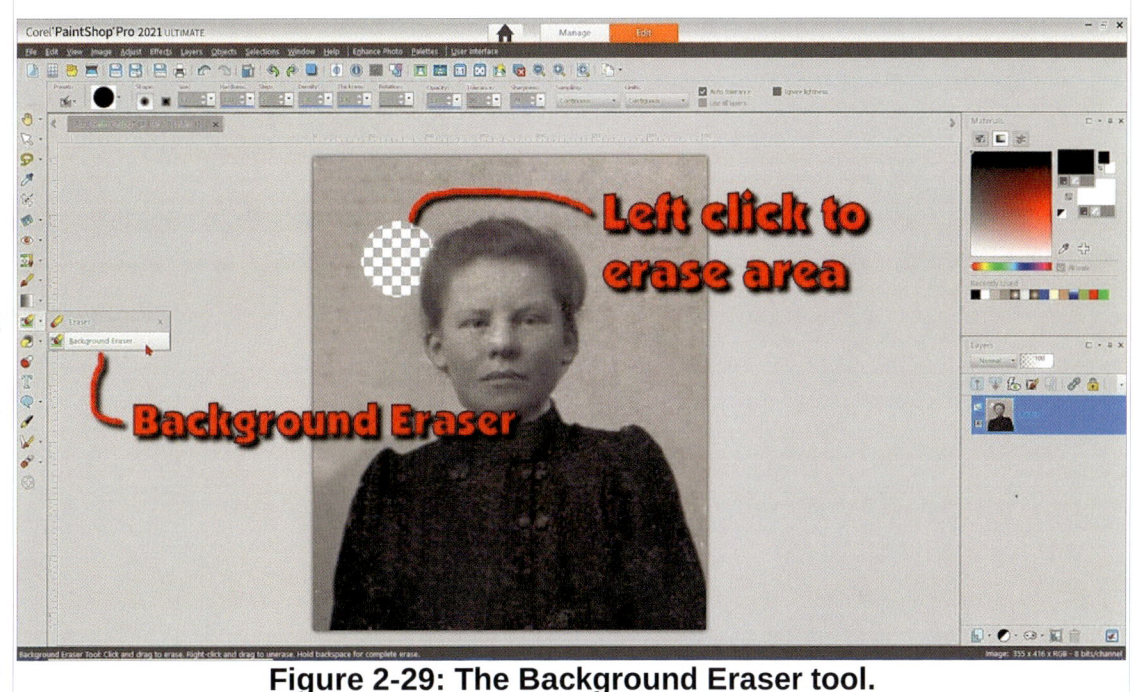

Figure 2-29: The Background Eraser tool.

Remember the **Ctrl+Z** shortcut for **Undo**. You will be using it frequently as you work you way around the photo. You will want to change the eraser size, and zoom in and out often. Watch the checkerboard pattern and clear up any breaks in the pattern. You can also click and drag to erase larger areas.

✓ Use the **Background Eraser** to clean up the area around Aunt Selma.

Page 43

Paint Shop Pro 2021 Fundamentals

The Background Eraser tool replaces the current pixels with a transparent area. It is possible to use Flood Fill to fill the transparent area with a color, gradient, or pattern fill. However, there is a good chance that the Background Eraser missed a few pixels here or there. So, we will do an intermediate step and flatten all layers. This will cause the transparent area to take on the current background color (by default it is white). Then we can go in with the Pain Brush tool and fine tune the photo.

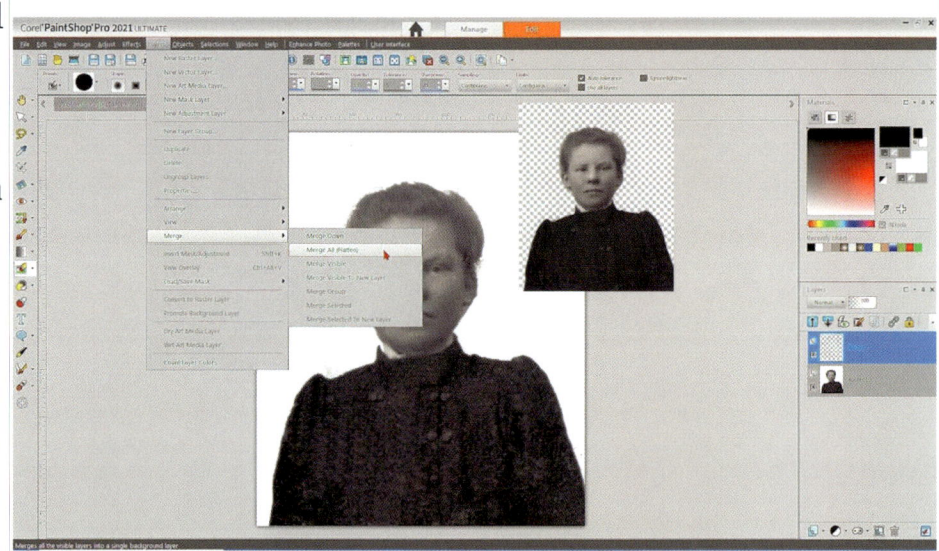

Figure 2-30: Merging Layers.

- ✔ Select **Layers, Merge, Merge All**.
- ✔ Use the **Paint Brush** tool to touch up any non white areas.
- ✔ Save the image as **Aunt Selma 3**.
- ✔ **Flood Fill** the background and Save As **Aunt Selma 4**.

Figure 2-31: Improving Aunt Selma photo.

Page 44

Part 2 – Enhancing Photos

The Object Remover Tool

To create the improved portrait of Aunt Selma, we used the cropping tool to capture a rectangular area. There is a better tool to use when the area to be isolated is not rectangular. The **Object Remover** tool provides for freehand drawing a border around the desired area.

Figure 2-33 shows that the **Object Remover** tool has been used to capture Grandpa Nasman. Once an area has been captured (selected) it can be copied and pasted as a new image.

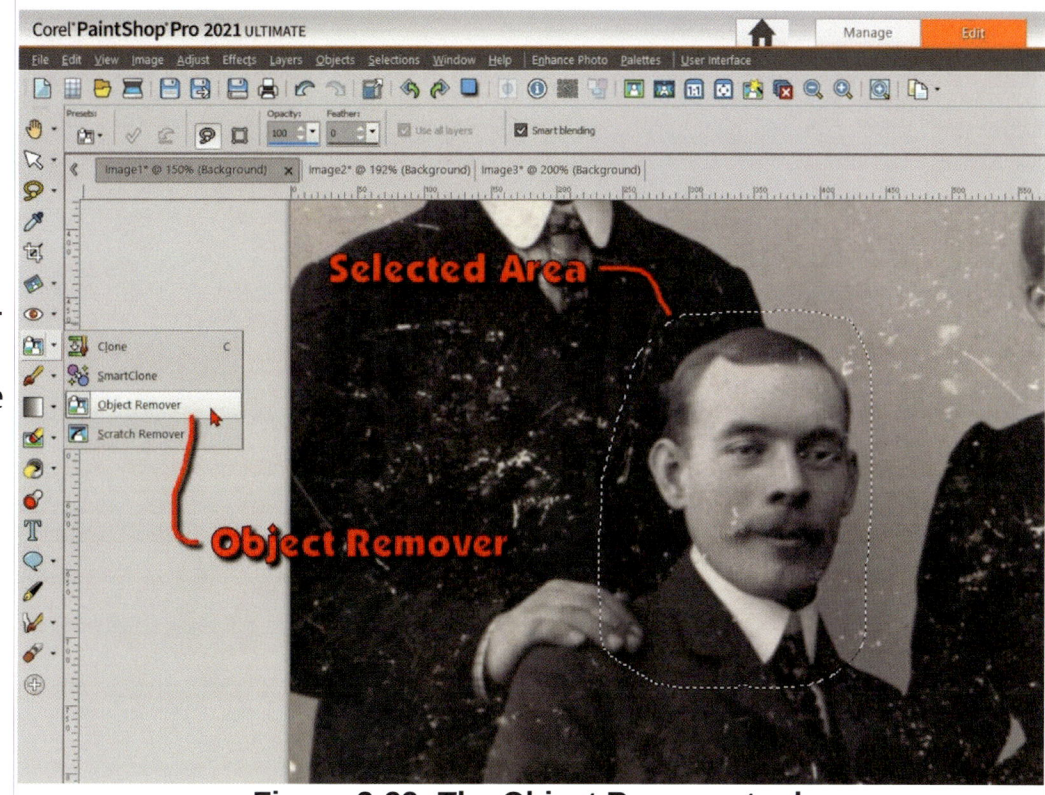

Figure 2-32: The Object Remover tool.

- Use the **Object Remover** tool to capture **Grandpa Nasman**.
- Select **Edit, Copy** to copy the selection to the clipboard.
- Select **Edit, Paste As New Image**.
- Select **File, Save As** and enter **Grandpa Nasman** as the file name.
- Use the **Clone** tool and **Paint Brush** tools to retouch the Grandpa Nasman photo.
- Paint the *background* around Grandpa Nasman **white**.

Figure 33: Improved Grandpa Nasman.

Let's have a little fun with the Grandpa Nasman portrait. First, we will add more white around the image.

- With the Grandpa Nasman image open, select **Image, Add Borders**.

Paint Shop Pro 2021 Fundamentals

- Set the border color to **white**, and the size to **50**.

This adds more space around the image for the next step.

The **Flood Fill** tool can be used to change the white background. You should experiment with different backgrounds until you find one you like.

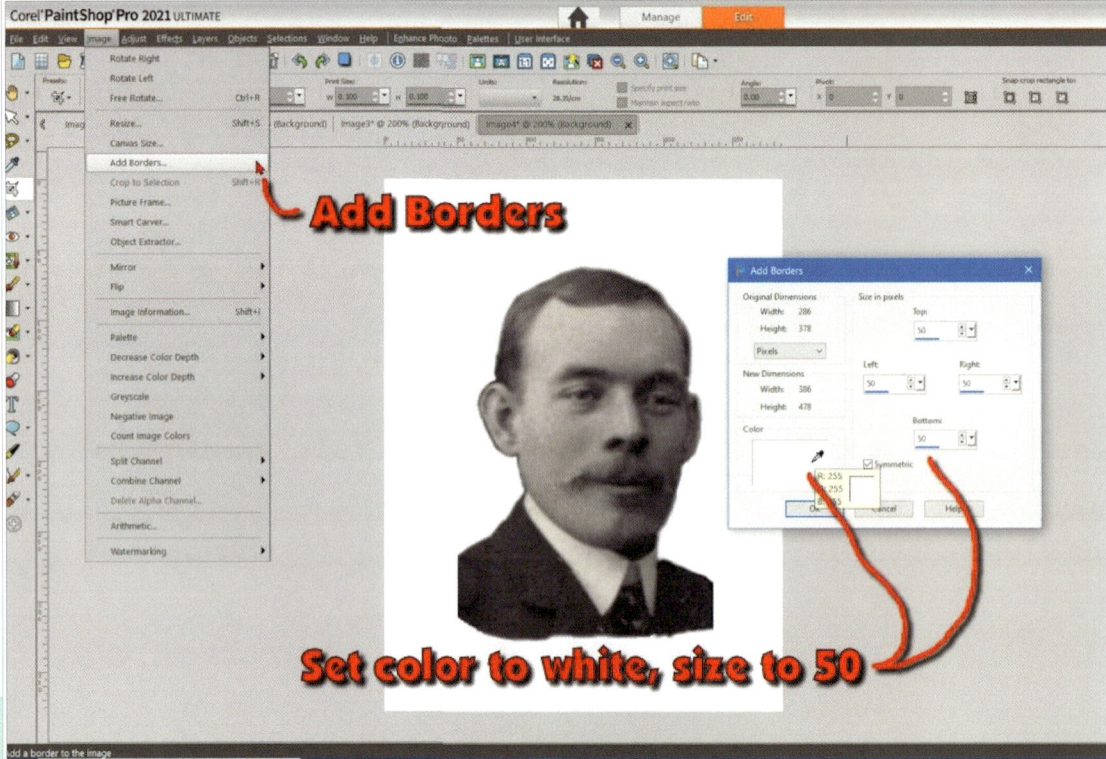

Figure 2-34: Adding a border.

- Select the **Flood Fill** tool and then choose a gradient (or whatever you prefer) and fill the **background** of the image.
- Go a little crazy and experiment with different **backgrounds** and **frames**.

With a little effort (or maybe a lot of effort) you can rescue old photos, and even make new photos from old ones.

Figure 2-35: Retouched photos.

Part 2 – Enhancing Photos

Here is a retouching challenge for you.

- From the practice images PDF file, Select the **Figure 11, Family 5** image from the PDF file. image, *right click*, and then select **Copy Image**.
- Use the *Taskbar* or press *Alt+tab* and switch to Paint Shop Pro window.
- From the Paint Shop Pro *Menubar*, select **Edit, Paste as New Image** [or, press **Shift+Insert**].

Figure 2-37: Retouching Challenge.

- Create a framed picture of Lucille similar to that shown in Figure 2-37.

Hints:

➢ Use a combination of the **Background Eraser** tool and the **Eraser Tool** to remove he unwanted background.
➢ Flood fill the area around the picture.
➢ Use multiple Picture Frame options to create a portrait version. (The Gold Frame was applied twice in he example to add more depth to the frame.)

Paint Shop Pro 2021 Fundamentals

Retouching Challenges

Page 48

Part 3 - Printing

Printing Images

Paint Shop Pro provides a variety of tools to help with printing. You can print a single image sized to fit a page, or scaled to a specified size. Templates are available for printing multiple images on a page.

The Print Dialog Box Options.

Figure 3-1 shows the Print dialog box with the **Placement** tab selected. It also shows the framed Grandpa Nasman image was active before the Print tool was selected.

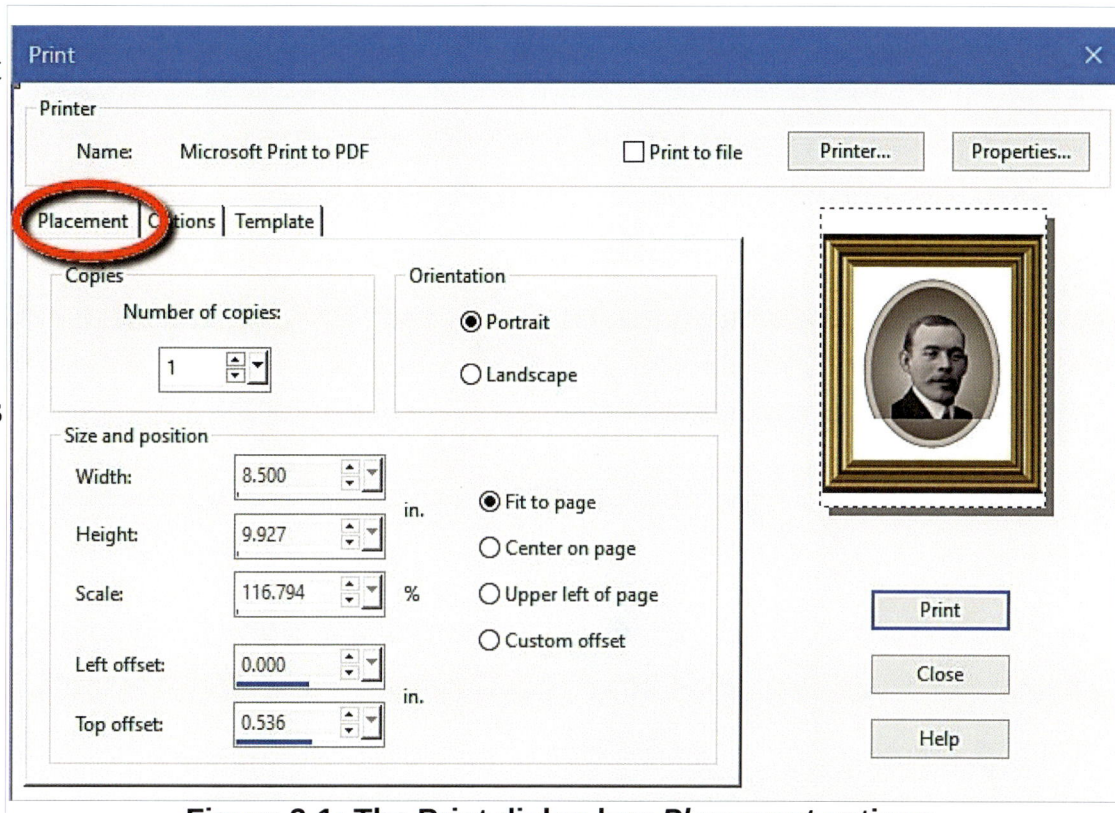

Figure 3-1: The Print dialog box *Placement* options.

- ✔ Select **File, Print** [or press **Ctrl+P**] to open the **Print Dialog box**.
- ✔ Observe the Print dialog box **Placement** options.

➢ There are buttons in the upper right of the dialog box for selecting the **printer** and adjusting the **printer properties**.

➢ There is a drop down text box for selecting the number of copies. The orientation of the page can be set to either **Portrait** or **Landscape**.

➢ When the **Fit to page option** is toggled **ON**, the **Size and position** values are not available. The Size and position values are available for the other options.

➢ When the printer dialog box options are set as desired, selection the **Print** button will send the page to the printer.

Page 49

Paint Shop Pro 2021 Fundamentals

Figure 3-2 shows the Print dialog box with the **Options** tab selected. It also shows that the framed Grandpa Nasman image was active before the Print tool was selected.

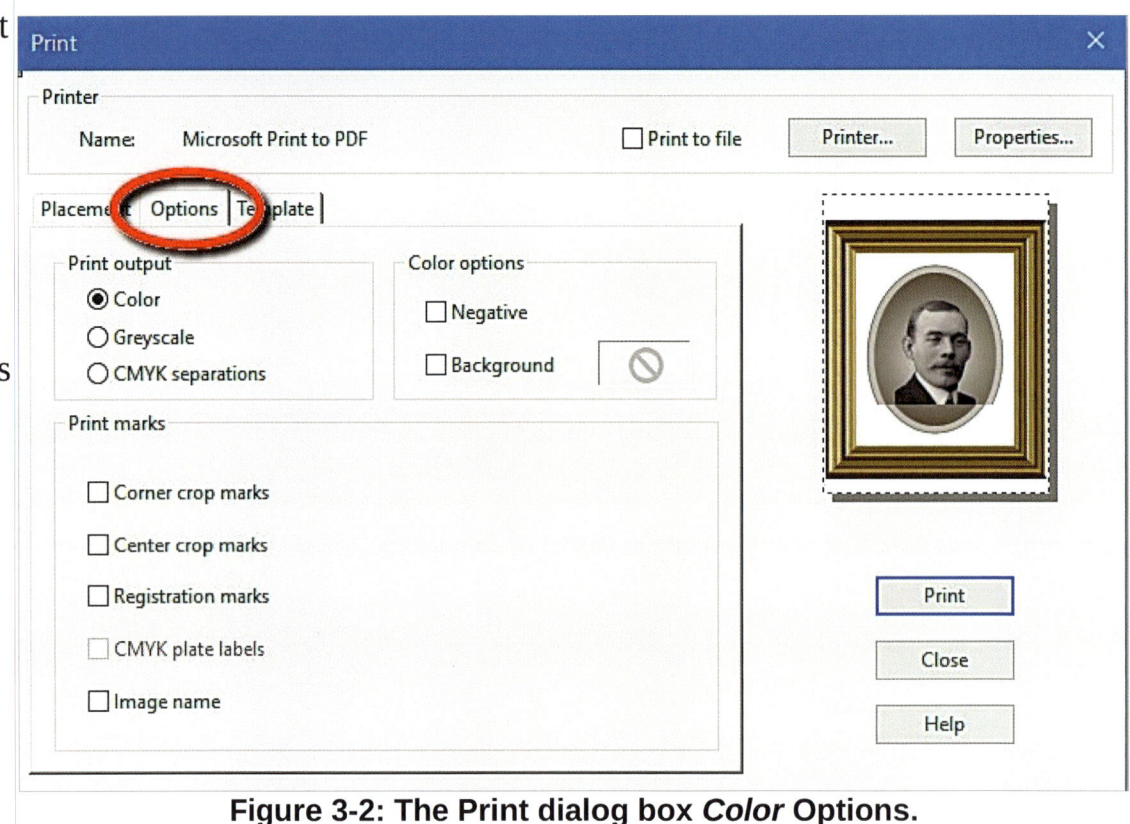

Figure 3-2: The Print dialog box *Color* Options.

- Observe the Print dialog box **Color** options.
  - The **Print output** can be switched between **Color, Greyscale**, and **CMYK separations.**
  - Colors can be printed as **Negative**.
  - **Print marks**, such as crop marks, can be added to the print.

Page 50

Part 3 - Printing

Figure 3-3 shows the Print dialog box with the **Template** tab selected. It also shows the framed Aunt Selma image was active before the Print tool was selected.

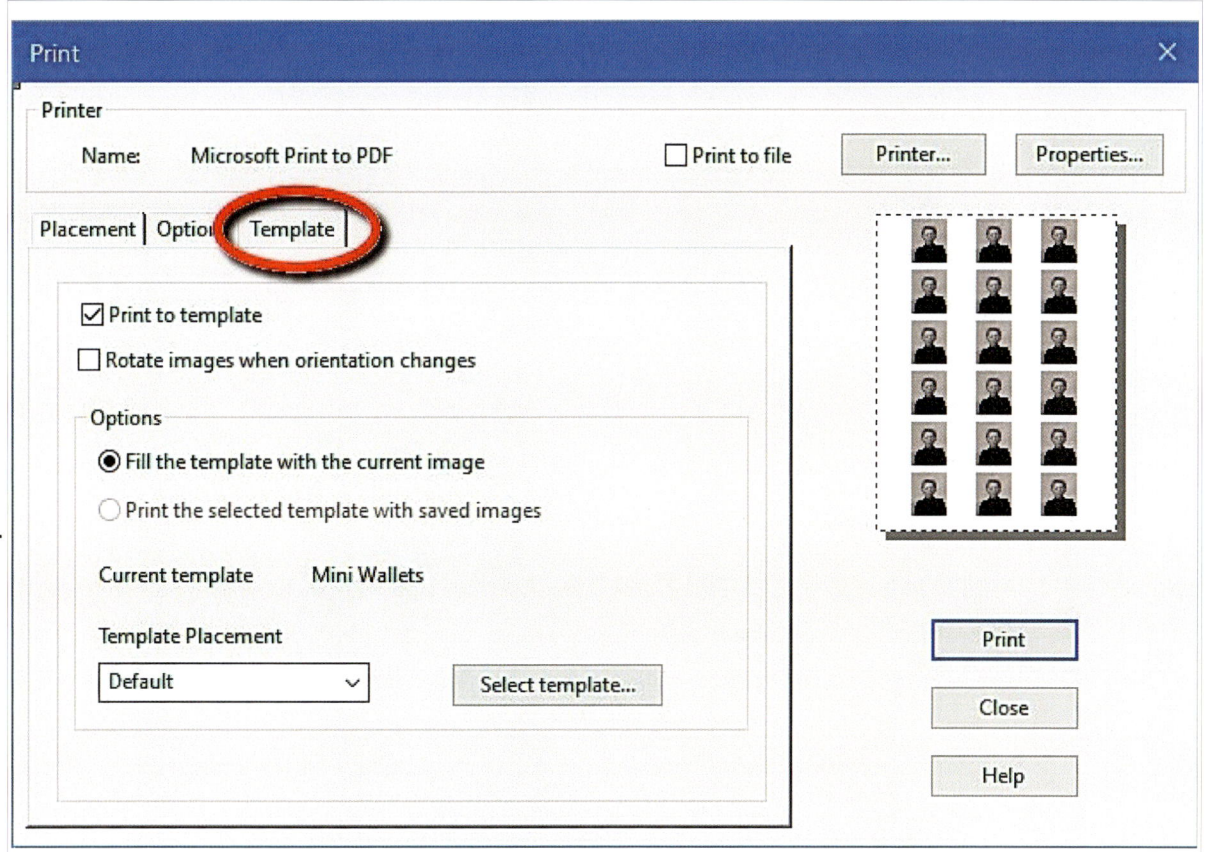

Figure 3-3: The Print dialog box *Template* Options.

✔ Observe the Print dialog box **Template** options.

> The **Print to template** toggle will open template options.

Figure 3-4 shows standard templates. There are other templates for Avery products.

Figure 3-3 shows that the **Mini Wallets** template was selected.

As you can see, Paint Shop Pro offers a wide variety of printing options. But wait, there is another way to control printer output.

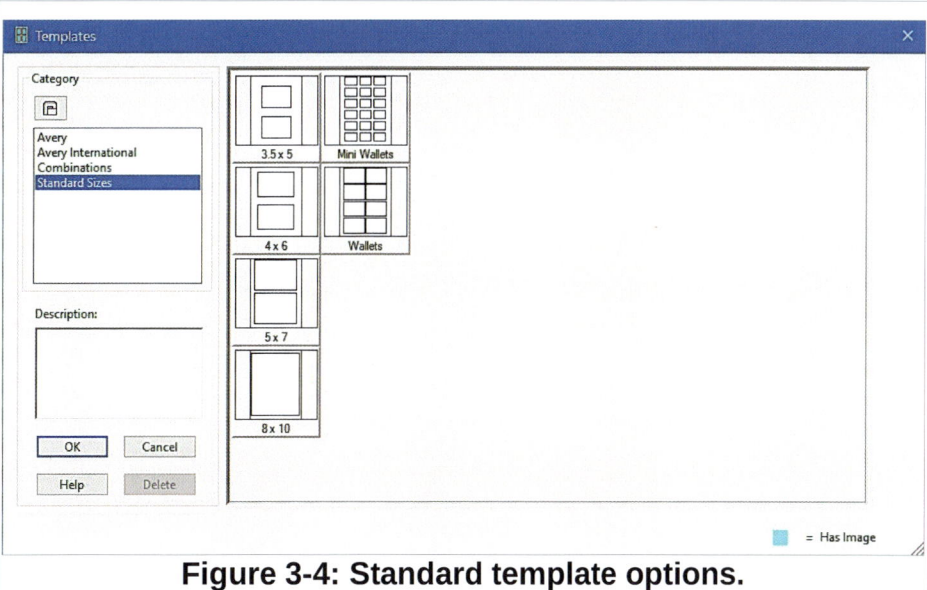

Figure 3-4: Standard template options.

Paint Shop Pro 2021 Fundamentals

Custom Print Layouts

✓ With several images open, select **File, Print Layout**.

Figure 3-5 shows a layout with three open images. Each of the pictures was dragged to the page, resized, and dragged into position.

➢ The **Print Layout toolbar** provides a collection of different tools to explore. One of the options is to add text to the layout.

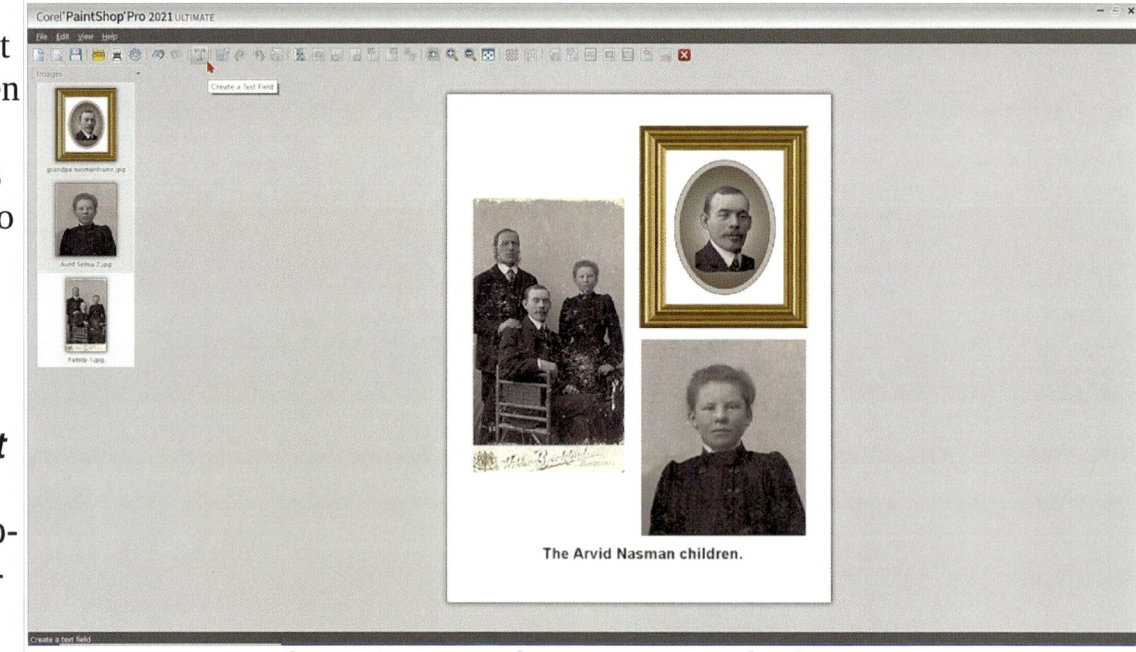

Figure 3-5: Creating a custom print layout.

✓ Explore the **Custom Print Layout** tools.

➢ One of the **Custom Print Layout** tools will open the preset layout collection seen earlier on the Print dialog box.

➢ Another **Custom Print Layout** tool allows for **saving** custom layouts.

Part 4 - Customizing The Interface, And Tips And Tricks

Creating A Custom Toolbar and Workspace.

You can customize the toolbar by adding and removing tool icons. It is possible to create customized toolbars (and Workspaces) for each type of work you do.

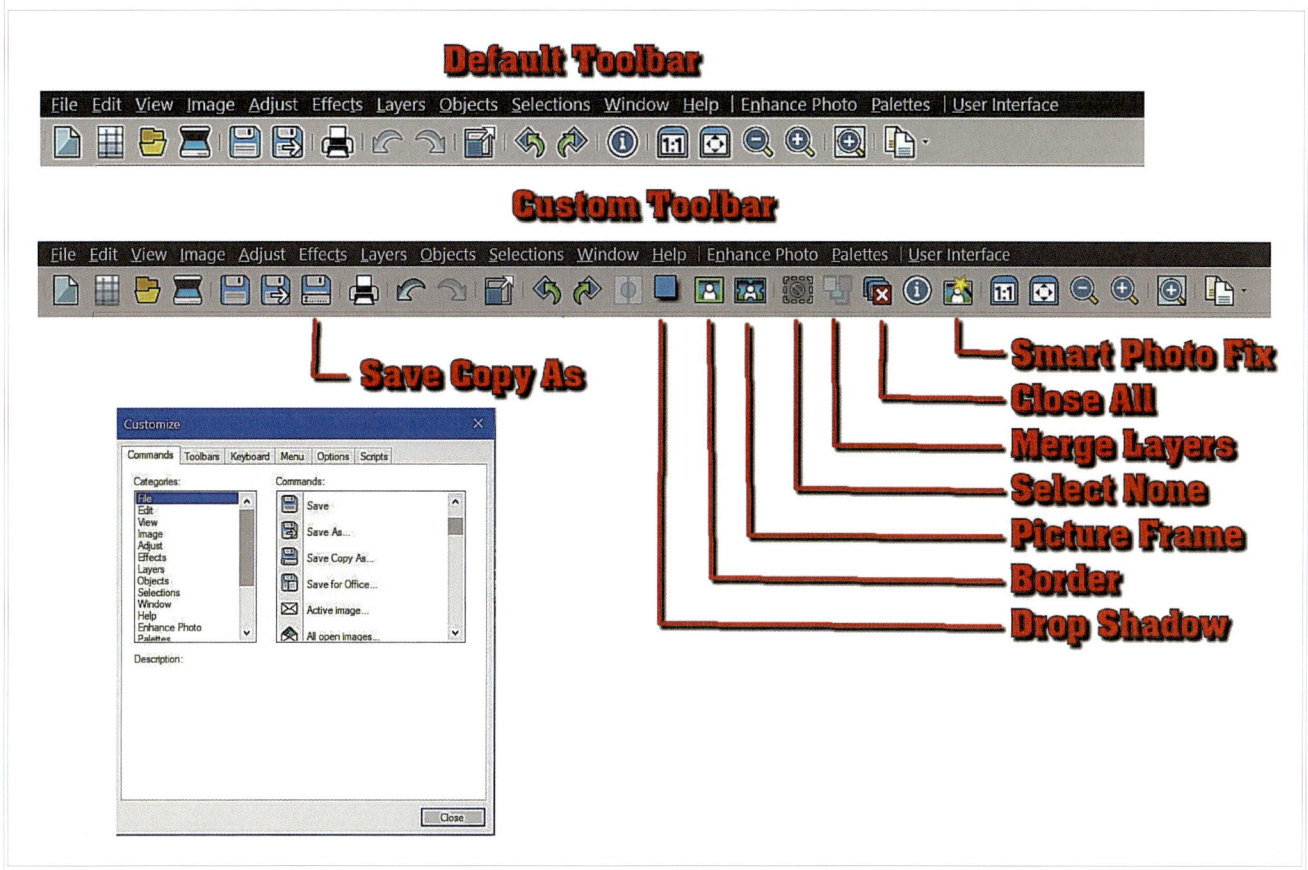

Figure 4-1: A Custom Toolbar.

Figure 4-1 shows the Default Toolbar, and a Custom Toolbar with the additional tools identified. The custom toolbar has tools that were frequently used while preparing this tutorial.

The toolbar is customized by dragging tool icons from The Customize dialog box to the toolbar.

- ✔ To open the **Customize** dialog box, **right click** just to the right of the toolbar, then select **Customize** from the context menu.
- ✔ Select the **File** option in the Customize dialog box, then **drag** the **Save Copy As** tool to the **toolbar**.
- ✔ Repeat the process of dragging tools to the toolbar until you have added the tools shown (or your most commonly used tools).

Paint Shop Pro 2021 Fundamentals

Saving A Workspace

Workspaces contain custom toolbars. They can also include images. This means that if you frequently start with a specific image, for a new drawing or other image file, you can create a workspace that includes that image. This means that every time you start Paint Shop Pro, it will open with your custom toolbar and image.

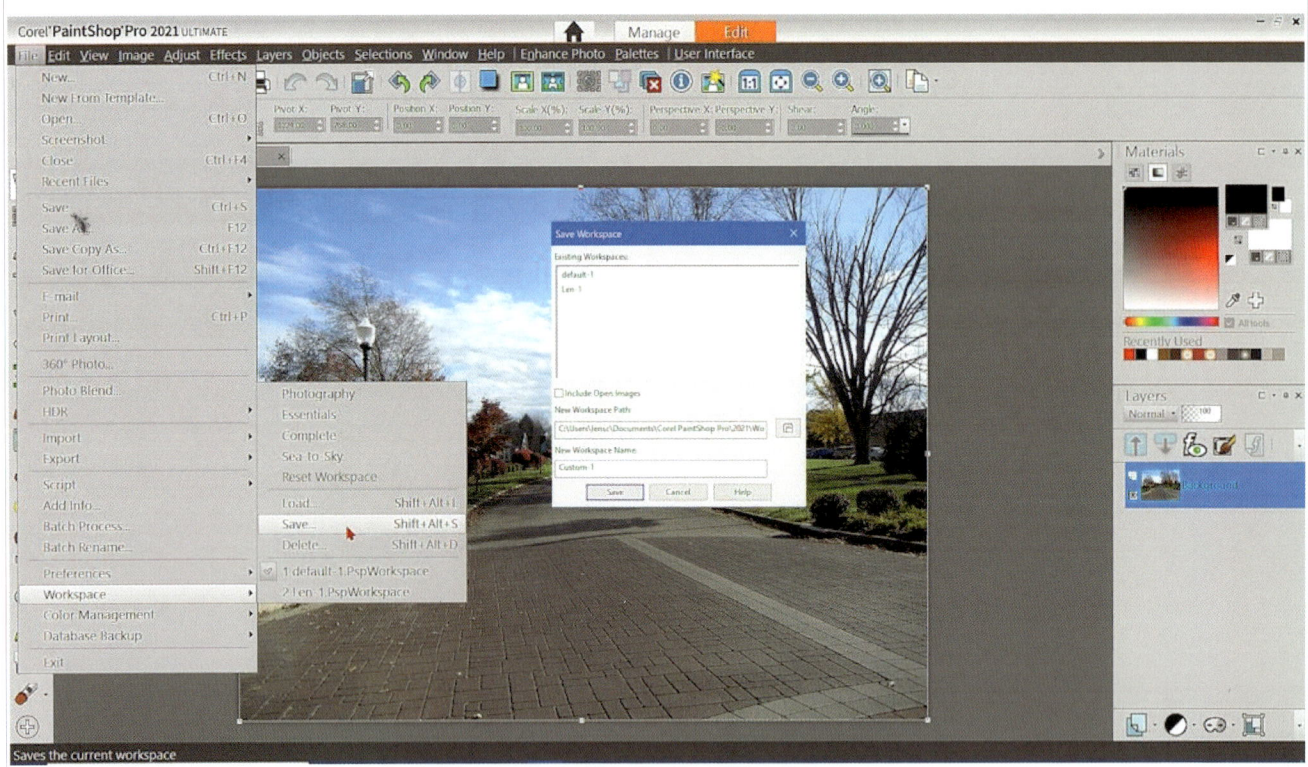

Figure 4-2: Saving a Workspace.

- From the **Menubar**, select **File, Workspace, Save**.
- Enter the **name** for your custom workspace in the **Save Workspace** dialog box.

Part 4 - Customizing The Interface, And Tips And Tricks

Tips and Tricks

Here are some tips and tricks that can help you work faster and more effectively with Paint Shop Pro 2021.

- Use the shortcuts **Ctrl+C** to *copy* and **Ctrl+V** to *paste*. You can copy text and images from any open documents, including Internet web pages, and paste them into Paint Shop Pro images.
- Create a **Custom Toolbar** that includes your frequently used tools.
- Create **Custom Workspaces** for each type of project you work on.
- Use the **Dropper** tool to select foreground or background colors from an open image. Position the cursor over the desired color area in an image, then *left click* to make this be the foreground color, or *right click* to make this be the background color.
- Use the **Selection** tool to select part of the open image. Observe that there are five different selection tool options. When a selection has been made it can be:
  - dragged to a new location
  - deleted (when a selection is **deleted**, it will be replaced by the current background color)
  - copied (Ctrl+C) to the clipboard. Select Menubar, Edit to control what happens to clipboard images.
- Use the **Pick** tool to select an object.
- Use the **Grab Points** to resize a selected object.
- To dynamically *resize* a brush, hold the **Alt key** down while dragging the mouse.

This version was edited May 6, 2021

Printed in Great Britain
by Amazon